Tolley's Capital Gains Tax 2017
Post-Budget Supplement

Tolley's Capital Gains Tax 2017 Post-Budget Supplement

by
Kevin Walton MA

Members of the LexisNexis Group worldwide

United Kingdom	RELX (UK) Limited trading as LexisNexis, 1–3 Strand, London WC2N 5JR
Australia	Reed International Books Australia Pty Ltd trading as LexisNexis, Chatswood, New South Wales
Austria	LexisNexis Verlag ARD Orac GmbH & Co KG, Vienna
Benelux	LexisNexis Benelux, Amsterdam
Canada	LexisNexis Canada, Markham, Ontario
China	LexisNexis China, Beijing and Shanghai
France	LexisNexis SA, Paris
Germany	LexisNexis Deutschland GmbH, Munster
Hong Kong	LexisNexis Hong Kong, Hong Kong
India	LexisNexis India, New Delhi
Italy	Giuffrè Editore, Milan
Japan	LexisNexis Japan, Tokyo
Malaysia	Malayan Law Journal Sdn Bhd, Kuala Lumpur
Mexico	LexisNexis Mexico, Mexico
New Zealand	LexisNexis NZ Ltd, Wellington
Singapore	LexisNexis Singapore, Singapore
South Africa	LexisNexis Butterworths, Durban
USA	LexisNexis, Dayton, Ohio

© 2017 RELX (UK) Limited.

Published by Lexis Nexis
This is a Tolley title

ISBN for this volume: 9780754553687

Printed and bound in Great Britain by Hobbs the Printers Ltd, Totton, Hampshire.

Visit LexisNexis at www.lexisnexis.co.uk

About This Supplement

This Supplement to Tolley's Capital Gains Tax 2016/17 gives details of changes in the law and practice of capital gains tax and corporation tax on chargeable gains from 2 September 2016 to 7 March 2017. It lists the changes in the same order and under the same paragraph headings as the annual publication. Also included is a summary of the Chancellor's Budget proposals made on 8 March 2017.

Each time Tolley's Capital Gains Tax 2016/17 is used, reference should be made to the material contained in this Supplement. The Contents gives a list of all the chapters and paragraphs which have been updated.

Contents

4   **Anti-Avoidance**

Approach of the Courts   **4.2**

General anti-abuse rule   **4.3**

Accelerated payment notices   **4.29**

Serial avoiders regime   **4.32**

5   **Appeals**

Failure to comply with rules   **5.13**

Award of costs   **5.24**

6   **Assessments**

Discovery assessments   **6.10**

7   **Assets**

Options   **7.7**

11   **Charities**

Gift aid donations by individuals   **11.10**

Community amateur sports clubs   **11.12**

16   **Computation of Gains and Losses**

Disposal   **16.3**

21   **Double Tax Relief**

Current agreements   **21.3**

22   **Employee Share Schemes**

Employee shareholder shares   **22.26**

23   **Enterprise Investment Scheme**

General requirements   **23.3**

24   **Entrepreneurs' Relief**

Introduction to entrepreneurs' relief   **24.1**

25   **Exemptions and Reliefs**

Child Trust Funds   **25.24**

Individual Savings Accounts (ISAs)   **25.30**

28   **Government Securities**

Exempt securities   **28.2**

29   **Groups of Companies**

Change of a company's nature   **29.21A**

31   **HMRC — Confidentiality of Information**

Introduction   **31.1**

	Publication of details of deliberate tax defaulters	**31.3**
32	**HMRC Explanatory Publications**	
	HMRC explanatory pamphlets	**32.1**
33	**HMRC Extra-Statutory Concessions**	
	The concessions	**33.2**
34	**HMRC Investigatory Powers**	
	Contractual disclosure facility	**34.13**
	Data-gathering powers	**34.17**
37	**Incorporation and Disincorporation Reliefs**	
	Transfer of business to a company — incorporation relief	**37.2**
38	**Indexation**	
	Calculation of indexation allowance	**38.2**
	Disposals on a no gain/no loss basis	**38.4**
	Options	**38.8**
42	**Late Payment Interest and Penalties**	
	Late payment interest (the new regime)	**42.2**
	Companies	**42.7**
44	**Losses**	
	Profit and losses of theatre backers (angels)	**44.9**
	Assets of negligible value	**44.11**
	Losses on shares in unlisted trading companies — individuals	**44.15**
49	**Overseas Matters**	
	UK resident participator in overseas resident company	**49.7**
	Tax collection agreement with Switzerland	**49.22**
52	**Penalties**	
	Introduction to penalties	**52.1**
	Cross-tax penalty for failure to make returns	**52.5**
	Penalty for offshore asset moves	**52.12**
	Asset-based penalty for offshore inaccuracies and failures	**52.13**
	Failure to produce documents during enquiry	**52.15**
	Enabling offshore tax evasion	**52.20**
55	**Remittance Basis**	
	Introduction to the remittance basis	**55.1**

58   **Returns**

Introduction to returns   **58.1**

Completion of enquiry   **58.12**

65   **Social Investment Relief**

Introduction   **65.1**

66   **Substantial Shareholdings of Companies**

Introduction   **66.1**

Spring Budget 2017

4

Anti-Avoidance

Approach of the Courts

[4.2] The final paragraph under the heading 'The 'Ramsay' principle' is amended to read as follows.

'See also *Exors of Connell v HMRC* FTT, [2016] UKFTT 154 (TC); 2016 STI 1802 (market value of loan notes) and *Trustees of the Morrison 2002 Maintenance Trust v HMRC* FTT, [2016] SFTD 894 (disposal of shares by trustees involving intermediate sale to non-resident trust).'

General anti-abuse rule

[4.3] The following paragraph is added immediately before the heading 'Definitions'.

'HMRC do not give formal or informal clearances that the GAAR does not apply. As part of its engagement with large businesses and wealthy individuals, however, HMRC does discuss commercial arrangements and confirm where appropriate that it doesn't regard particular arrangements as tax avoidance. See www.gov.uk/government/collections/seeking-clearance-or-approval-for-a-t ransaction.'

Accelerated payment notices

[4.29] The final paragraph is amended to read as follows.

'Attempts to have the giving of an accelerated payment notice declared unlawful were unsuccessful in *R (oao Walapu) v HMRC* QB, [2016] STC 1682 and *R (oao Graham) v HMRC* QB 2016, [2017] STC 1. A judicial review application was unsuccessful in *Sword Services Ltd v HMRC* QB, [2016] EWHC 1473 (Admin); 2016 STI 1799.'

Serial avoiders regime

[4.32] The following text is added at the end of the third paragraph.

'For HMRC guidance see www.gov.uk/guidance/serial-tax-avoidance.'

5

Appeals

Failure to comply with rules

[5.13] The final paragraph under the heading 'Striking out a case' is amended to read as follows.

'An attempt to have HMRC barred from taking any part in a case was unsuccessful in *Foulser v HMRC* FTT 2011, [2012] SFTD 94. On appeal to the Upper Tribunal, however, the case was remitted for rehearing by the FTT ([2013] STC 917). An attempt to have HMRC barred also failed in *Ritchie v HMRC* FTT, [2016] UKFTT 509 (TC), [2016] STI 2753.'

Award of costs

[5.24] The penultimate paragraph is updated to read as follows.

'For the award of costs where HMRC successfully applied to admit late evidence see *Earthshine Ltd v HMRC* FTT, [2010] UKFTT 314 (TC); 2010 STI 2621. An application for costs arising from an application to have a case recategorised as complex was unsuccessful in *Capital Air Services Ltd v HMRC* UT, [2011] STC 617. Partially successful appellants were ordered to pay two-thirds of HMRC's costs in *Bastionspark LLP v HMRC* UT, [2016] STC 2549.'

6

Assessments

Discovery assessments

[6.10] The final case reference in the paragraph beginning 'In *Charlton v HMRC* . . . ' is updated to *Pattullo v HMRC (No 2)* UT, [2016] STC 2043.

The case reference in the paragraph beginning 'In *Anderson v HMRC* . . . ' is updated to *Anderson v HMRC* FTT 2016, [2017] SFTD 100.

7

Assets

Options

[7.7] The paragraph immediately before the heading 'Exclusion' is amended to read as follows.

'An attempt to exploit *TCGA 1992, s 144ZA* as part of an avoidance scheme failed in *Trustees of the Morrison 2002 Maintenance Trust v HMRC* FTT, [2016] SFTD 894.'

11

Charities

Gift aid donations by individuals

[11.10] The paragraph headed 'The charity' is amended to read as follows.

'The receipt by a charity of a qualifying donation is treated as the receipt, under deduction of income tax at the basic rate for the tax year in which the gift is made, of an amount equal to the 'grossed up amount of the gift' (see (a) above). [*ITA 2007, s 520; CTA 2010, ss 471, 661D; FA 2012, Sch 15 para 6*]. An election by the donor to treat a qualifying donation as being made in the previous tax year does not affect the position of the charity; the donation is grossed up by reference to the basic rate for the tax year in which payment is *actually* made.'

The section headed 'Qualifying donations' is amended to read as follows.

'A '*qualifying donation*' is a gift to a charity by the donor which meets the following conditions:

(I)   it takes the form of a payment of a sum of money;
(II)   it is not subject to a condition as to repayment;
(III)   it is not deductible under the payroll deduction scheme — see Tolley's Income Tax under Charities);
(IV)   it is not deductible in calculating the donor's income from any source;
(V)   it is not conditional on or associated with, or part of an arrangement involving, the acquisition of property by the charity, otherwise than by way of gift, from the donor or a person connected with him;
(VI)   neither the donor nor any person connected with him (see **17** CONNECTED PERSONS) receives any benefit, in consequence of making it, in excess of specified limits (see below); and
(VII)   the donor or, for donations made on or after 6 April 2017, an 'intermediary' representing the donor gives the charity or, for donations on or after the same date, an intermediary representing the charity, a 'gift aid declaration' in relation to it.

A gift to charity is also a '*qualifying donation*' if it meets the conditions above and the payment is by way of a waiver by the individual of entitlement to sums (whether principal or interest) due to him from the charity in respect of an amount advanced to the charity on which social investment income tax relief has been obtained (see **65** SOCIAL INVESTMENT RELIEF).

A '*gift aid declaration*' for the purposes of (VII) above is a declaration which is given in the manner prescribed by regulations. It may be made in writing, by fax, over the internet or orally (e.g. by telephone). It must contain the donor's name and address, the name of the charity, a description of the gift(s) to which it relates and a statement that the gift(s) is (are) to be treated as qualifying donations for these purposes. In order for the declaration to have effect, it must have been explained to the donor that he must pay sufficient income tax or capital gains tax to cover the tax deemed to be deducted at source from the donation. No signature is required. Charities and intermediaries must maintain a satisfactory auditable (by HMRC) record of declarations given to them. A donor may still cancel the donation of his own volition. An *'intermediary'* is a person authorised by the donor to give a declaration on his behalf to the charity; a person authorised by a charity to receive a declaration on its behalf; or a person authorised to perform both of those roles. Penalties may be imposed on charities and intermediaries who fail to comply with the regulations.

[*ITA 2007, ss 416, 417, 422, 428; FA 2012, s 50(3)(b); FA 2014, Sch 11 para 11; FA 2015, s 20; FA 2016, s 173; SI 2000 No 2074; SI 2005 No 2790; SI 2016 Nos 1010, 1195*].

As regards (VI) above, the benefit does not have to be received from the charity to be taken into account (see *St Dunstan's v Major* (Sp C 127), [1997] SSCD 212, in which the saving of inheritance tax by personal representatives as a result of the variation of a will to provide for a donation which would otherwise qualify under these provisions constituted a benefit).

The release of a loan not for consideration and not under seal cannot amount to a gift of money (see *Battle Baptist Church v CIR and Woodham* (Sp C 23), [1995] SSCD 176).'

Community amateur sports clubs

[11.12] The list on page 240 is amended to read as follows.

'A club is *'organised on an amateur basis'* if it meets the following four conditions.

(a)   The club must be non-profit making, i.e. its constitution must require surplus income or gains to be reinvested in the club and must not permit the distribution of club assets (whether in cash or in kind) to members or third parties. However, donations by a club to charities or other registered clubs are allowed.

(b)   It must provide only the following benefits for members and their guests:
   –   provision of sporting facilities and suitably qualified coaches;
   –   reasonable provision and maintenance of club-owned sports equipment;
   –   provision of, or reimbursement of the costs of, coaching courses;
   –   provision of insurance cover and medical treatment;
   –   reimbursement of reasonable and, with effect from 1 April 2015, necessary travel or subsistence expenses incurred by players, match officials and, with effect from 1 April 2015, coaches, first aiders and accompanying individuals travelling to away matches;
   –   reasonable provision of post-match refreshments for players and match officials; and
   –   sale or supply of food or drink as a social adjunct to the sporting purposes of the club.

(c)   It does not exceed the limit on paid players. The limit is, broadly, £10,000 per year. For the detailed rules see *SI 2015 No 725, Regs 11–13*.

(d) The club's constitution must provide for any net assets on the dissolution of the club to be applied for the purposes of:
  – a charity;
  – another registered club; or
  – the governing body of an eligible sport for the purposes of which the club existed, for use in related community sport,
  as approved by the members of the club in general meeting or by its governing body.'

The last four paragraphs before the heading 'Registration' are amended to read as follows.

'A club meets the management condition if its managers are fit and proper persons. For this purpose, the managers are the persons with the general control and management of the administration of the club. If this condition is not met for a period of time it is nevertheless treated as met throughout that period if HMRC consider either that the failure has not prejudiced the purposes of the club or that it is just and reasonable for the condition to be treated as met. The expression 'fit and proper' is not defined and so takes its natural meaning. HMRC consider that the fit and proper person test is the same as that for charities (see **11.2** above).

A club meets the income condition if the total of its trading receipts and property receipts does not exceed £100,000 for an accounting period. The limit is reduced proportionately where the accounting period is less than 12 months. The receipts taken into account are those that would be included in computing the club's trading income and property income for corporation tax if the exemptions for such income did not apply.

[CTA 2010, ss 658(1)–(1C), 659–661CA; FA 2012, s 52; FA 2013, Sch 21; SI 2010 No 1904; SI 2014 No 1807; SI 2015 Nos 674, 725].

For HMRC guidance on eligibility conditions see www.gov.uk/government/p ublications/community-amateur-sports-clubs-detailed-guidance-notes/commu nity-amateur-sports-clubs-detailed-guidance-notes.'

The last two paragraphs under the heading 'Registration' are amended to read as follows.

'HMRC publishes the names and addresses of registered clubs. This enables potential donors to confirm that they are donating to a registered club (and, therefore, that the donation may qualify for gift aid relief — see below). For a list of the names of registered clubs see www.gov.uk/government/publication s/community-amateur-sports-clubs-casc-registered-with-hmrc--2.

[CTA 2010, ss 658(2)–(5), 670, 671].'

The section headed 'Tax exemptions' is updated to read as follows.

'Subject to the restriction noted below, a gain accruing to a registered club is not a chargeable gain if it is wholly applied for 'qualifying purposes' and the club makes a claim to that effect. '*Qualifying purposes*' means purposes of providing facilities for, and promoting participation in, one or more eligible sports (and in the following paragraphs, '*non-qualifying purposes*' are to be construed accordingly). [CTA 2010, ss 661(3), 665].

In addition to the exemption for gains, registered clubs also enjoy tax exemptions relating to trading income, interest and gift aid income and property income. For full details, see Tolley's Corporation Tax under Voluntary Associations.'

16
Computation of Gains and Losses

Disposal

[16.3] The case reference in the paragraph beginning 'In *Hardy v HMRC* . . . ' is updated to *Hardy v HMRC* UT, [2016] UKUT 349 (TCC), [2016] STI 2592.

21
Double Tax Relief

Current agreements

[21.3] The text from the beginning to the heading 'Czechoslovakia' is updated to read as follows.

'A list is given below of the double tax agreements made by the UK which are currently operative. The agreements have effect to the extent, and as from the operative dates, specified therein (SI numbers in round brackets). Additional notes for certain agreements are given after the list, together with details of agreements made but not yet in force.

Albania (2013/3145), **Antigua and Barbuda** (1947/2865; 1968/1096), **Argentina** (1997/1777), **Armenia** (2011/2722), **Australia** (1968/305; 1980/707; 2003/3199), **Austria** (1970/1947; 1979/117; 1994/768; 2010/2688), **Azerbaijan** (1995/762),

Bahrain (2012/3075), **Bangladesh** (1980/708), **Barbados** (2012/3076), **Belarus** (1995/2706 — see notes below), **Belgium** (1987/2053; 2010/2979), **Belize** (1947/2866; 1968/573; 1973/2097), **Bolivia** (1995/2707), **Bosnia-Herzegovina** (see note below), **Botswana** (2006/1925), **British Virgin Islands** (2009/3013), **Brunei** (1950/1977; 1968/306; 1973/2098; 2013/3146), **Bulgaria** (2015/1891; 1987/2054), **Burma** (see Myanmar below),

Canada (1980/709; 1980/1528; 1985/1996; 2003/2619; 2014/3274; 2015/2011), **Cayman Islands** (2010/2973), **Chile** (2003/3200), **China** (2011/2724; 2013/3142), **Croatia** (2015/2011), **Cyprus** (1975/425; 1980/1529), **Czech Republic** (see note below),

Denmark (1980/1960; 1991/2877; 1996/3165),

Egypt (1980/1091), Estonia (1994/3207), Ethiopia (2011/2725),

Falkland Islands (1997/2985), Faroe Islands (2007/3469; 1961/579; 1971/717; 1975/2190 until 6 April 1997), Fiji (1976/1342), Finland (1970/153; 1980/710; 1985/1997; 1991/2878; 1996/3166), France (2009/226),

Gambia (1980/1963), Georgia (2004/3325; 2010/2972), Germany (2010/2975; 1967/25; 1971/874; 2014/1874), Ghana (1993/1800), Greece (1954/142), Grenada (1949/361; 1968/1867), Guernsey (1952/1215; 1994/3209; 2015/2008; 2016/750), Guyana (1992/3207),

Hong Kong (2010/2974), Hungary (2011/2726),

Iceland (2014/1879; 1991/2879), India (1981/1120; 1993/1801; 2013/3147), Indonesia (1994/769), Ireland (1976/2151, 1976/2152; 1995/764; 1998/3151), Isle of Man (1955/1205; 1991/2880; 1994/3208; 2009/228; 2013/3148; 2016/749), Israel (1963/616; 1971/391), Italy (1990/2590), Ivory Coast (1987/169),

Jamaica (1973/1329), Japan (2006/1924; 2014/1881), Jersey (1952/1216; 1994/3210; 2015/2009; 2016/752), Jordan (2001/3924),

Kazakhstan (1994/3211; 1998/2567), Kenya (1977/1299), Kiribati (as per Tuvalu), Korea, Republic of (South) (1996/3168), Kosovo (2015/2007), Kuwait (1999/2036),

Latvia (1996/3167), Lesotho (1997/2986), Libya (2010/243), Liechtenstein (2012/3077), Lithuania (2001/3925; 2002/2847), Luxembourg (1968/1100; 1980/567; 1984/364; 2010/237),

Macedonia (2007/2127), Malawi (1956/619; 1964/1401; 1968/1101; 1979/302), Malaysia (1997/2987; 2010/2971), Malta (1995/763), Mauritius (1981/1121; 1987/467; 2003/2620; 2011/2442), Mexico (1994/3212; 2010/2686), Moldova (2008/1795), Mongolia (1996/2598), Montserrat (1947/2869; 1968/576; 2011/1083), Morocco (1991/2881), Myanmar (1952/751),

Namibia (1962/2352; 1962/2788; 1967/1490), Netherlands (2009/227; 1980/1961; 1983/1902; 1990/2152; 2013/3143), New Zealand (1984/365; 2004/1274; 2008/1793), Nigeria (1987/2057), Norway (2013/3144; 1985/1998; 2000/3247),

Oman (1998/2568; 2010/2687),

Pakistan (1987/2058), Panama (2013/3149), Papua New Guinea (1991/2882), Philippines (1978/184), Poland (2006/3323), Portugal (1969/599),

Qatar (2010/241; 2011/1684),

Romania (1977/57), Russia (1994/3213),

Saudi Arabia (2008/1770), St. Christopher (St. Kitts) and Nevis (1947/2872), Senegal (2015/1892 — applies in the UK from 1 April 2016 for corporation tax purposes and from 6 April 2016 for capital gains tax purposes), **Serbia and Montenegro** (see note below), Sierra Leone (1947/2873; 1968/1104), Singapore (1997/2988; 2010/2685; 2012/3078), **Slovak Republic (Slovakia)** (see note below), **Slovenia** (2008/1796), **Solomon Islands** (1950/748; 1968/574; 1974/1270), **South Africa** (1969/864; 2002/3138; 2011/2441), **Spain** (2013/3152), **Sri Lanka** (1980/713), **Sudan** (1977/1719), **Swaziland** (1969/380), **Sweden** (2015/1891; 1984/366), **Switzerland** (1978/1408; 1982/714; 1994/3215; 2007/3465; 2010/2689),

Taiwan (2002/3137), **Tajikistan** (2014/3275), **Thailand** (1981/1546), **Trinidad and Tobago** (1983/1903), **Tunisia** (1984/133), **Turkey** (1988/932), **Tuvalu** (1950/750; 1968/309; 1974/1271),

Uganda (1952/1213; 1993/1802), **Ukraine** (1993/1803), **U.S.A.** (1980/568; 2002/2848), **USSR** (see note below), **Uzbekistan** (1994/770),

Venezuela (1996/2599), **Vietnam** (1994/3216),

Yugoslavia (1981/1815 and see note below),

Zambia (2014/1876; 1972/1721; 1981/1816), **Zimbabwe** (1982/1842).

Shipping & Air Transport only—Algeria (Air Transport only) (1984/362), Brazil (1968/572), Cameroon (Air Transport only) (1982/1841), Ethiopia (Air Transport only) (1977/1297 — now replaced by comprehensive agreement above), Hong Kong (Air Transport) (1998/2566), Hong Kong (Shipping Transport) (2000/3248), Iran (Air Transport only) (1960/2419), Jordan (1979/300), Lebanon (1964/278), Saudi Arabia (Air Transport only) (1994/767), Zaire (1977/1298).'

Agreements not yet in force

The paragraph is amended to read as follows.

'The Agreement with Belarus had not yet entered into force in August 2008 and was then considered unlikely to enter into force in the near future. (HMRC Double Taxation Relief Manual DT3300). A protocol to the agreement with Belgium was signed on 14 March 2014 (see *SI 2014 No 1875*). A comprehensive agreement with Algeria was signed on 18 February 2015 (see *SI 2015 No 1888*). A comprehensive agreement with Uruguay was signed on 24 February 2016 (see *SI 2016 No 753* — applies in the UK from 1 April 2017 for corporation tax purposes and from 6 April 2017 for capital gains tax purposes). A comprehensive agreement with the United Arab Emirates was signed on 12 April 2016 (see *SI 2016 No 754*). A comprehensive agreement with Turkmenistan was signed on 10 June 2016 (see *SI 2016 No 1217* — applies in the UK from 1 April 2017 for corporation tax purposes and from 6 April 2017 for capital gains tax purposes). A comprehensive agreement with Colombia was signed on 2 November 2016. A new agreement with Lesotho was signed on 3 November 2016.'

22

Employee Share Schemes

Employee shareholder shares

[22.26] The section is updated to read as follows.

'A special employment status, known as 'employee shareholder' status, was introduced by *Growth and Infrastructure Act 2013, s 31*. Employee shareholders are issued or allotted at least £2,000 worth of shares in consideration of an employee shareholder agreement. Subject to conditions, an income tax relief and capital gains tax exemption apply to the shares, as described below. The relief and exemption apply to shares received through the adoption of employee shareholder status on or after 1 September 2013. [*FA 2013, Sch 23 para 38; SI 2013 No 1755*]. Businesses wishing to award shares under an employee shareholder agreement may propose a share valuation to HMRC's Shares and Assets Valuation team in advance of the award (HMRC Employment-Related Shares & Securities Bulletin No. 10, September 2013). For official guidance on the CGT treatment of employee shareholder shares see www.gov.uk/government/publications/guidance-on-the-capital-gains-tax-treat ment-of-employee-shareholder-shares/guidance-on-the-capital-gains-tax-treat ment-of-employee-shareholder-shares.

After only being in effect for just over three years, the income tax, NIC and capital gains tax reliefs in relation to employee shareholder status are to be scrapped, as a precursor to the whole concept of employee shareholder status being abolished at some future point. This is in response to HMRC's findings that these reliefs are primarily being used for tax-planning purposes by wealthier employees rather than fulfilling their original objective which was to enable small companies to recruit without committing to a permanent workforce with full employment rights.

As announced at Autumn Statement 2016, the government will legislate in Finance Bill 2017 to withdraw the capital gains tax exemption and the income tax and NIC reliefs in respect of shares received as consideration for entering into most Employee Shareholder Status agreements. Agreements entered into before 1 December 2016, or before 2 December 2016 where independent advice was received before 1:30 pm on 23 November 2016, will retain their tax benefits.

The independent advice received by an individual before entering into an Employee Shareholder agreement continues to be tax-free.

These changes do not affect the reliefs available to the employer company.

See www.gov.uk/government/publications/income-tax-and-capital-gains-tax-e mployee-shareholder-status.'

23

Enterprise Investment Scheme

General requirements

[23.3] The case reference in the paragraph beginning 'In *Flix Innovations Ltd v HMRC* . . . ' is updated to *Flix Innovations Ltd v HMRC* UT, [2016] STC 2206.

24

Entrepreneurs' Relief

Introduction to entrepreneurs' relief

[24.1] The following paragraph is added at the end.

'HMRC have identified an avoidance scheme which seeks to convert employment income into a capital gain eligible for entrepreneurs' relief. HMRC intend to challenge the scheme. See www.gov.uk/guidance/capital-gains-tax-entrepreneurs-relief-tax-avoidance-scheme.'

25

Exemptions and Reliefs

Child Trust Funds

[25.24] The section is updated to read as follows.

'The Child Trust Fund scheme is a government assisted savings scheme for any child born after 31 August 2002 and before 3 January 2011 where, broadly, there is an entitlement to child benefit (an '*eligible child*'). The scheme provides for HMRC to make an initial contribution in the form of a voucher (initially worth £250, or £500 for children in lower income families), which is then used to open an account. Anyone, including the child, may then pay money into the account up to a yearly limit of £4,128 (£4,080 before 6 April 2017; £4,000 before 6 April 2015; £3,840 before 1 July 2014; £3,600 before 6 April 2014 and £1,200 before 1 November 2011). For children born before 3 August 2010 HMRC make a further contribution when the child reaches the age of seven. For 2010/11 a further government contribution was made to the accounts of disabled children. Government contributions of all kinds have, however, been phased out. For children born in the period 4 August 2010 to

2 January 2011 the initial contribution was £50 or £100. Disabled contributions ceased for 2011/12 onwards. Children born from 3 January 2011 onwards do not qualify for a child trust fund. Existing funds, however, continue to maturity and non-government contributions continue to be permitted. With effect from 6 April 2015 it is possible to transfer a child trust fund to a junior ISA.

The account provider, acting on the instructions of a nominated responsible person (the *'registered contact'*), or the child if over 16, invests the funds in a limited range of qualifying investments. Normally no withdrawals are permitted before the fund matures when the child reaches 18. For further details see Tolley's Income Tax.

Tax treatment

No tax is chargeable in respect of interest, dividends, distributions, gains, alternative financial arrangement return or building society bonus on account investments. Capital losses on account investments are disregarded. Any income from account investments is not to be regarded as income for any income tax purposes. For capital gains tax purposes, any assets held as account investments are regarded as held by the child concerned in a separate capacity from that in which he holds any other assets of the same description. The child is treated as having sold all the account investments, and as having reacquired them in his personal capacity, for their market value immediately before attaining the age of 18.

It is up to the account provider to make tax claims, conduct appeals, and agree liabilities and reliefs on behalf of the child or registered contact. It is unlikely therefore that the child or registered contact will have to deal with any tax matters arising from the account. However, there is power for HMRC to make an assessment as an alternative to the account provider in order to withdraw relief or recover tax.

[*Child Trust Funds Act 2004, s 13; SI 2004 No 1450, Regs 24–38; SI 2005 No 3349; SI 2006 No 3195; SI 2010 No 1894; SI 2011 No 2447; SI 2012 No 1870; SI 2013 No 1744; SI 2014 Nos 649, 1453; SI 2015 Nos 876, 1371; SI 2017 No 185*].'

Individual Savings Accounts (ISAs)

[25.30] The text from the beginning to the heading 'eligibility' is replaced by the following.

'ISAs are available to individuals over 18 (though see below) who are both resident and ordinarily resident in the UK. The accounts can be made up of cash, stocks and shares and, after 5 April 2016, innovative finance (i.e., broadly, peer-to-peer loans made through a regulated peer-to-peer lending platform). For 2017/18, investors can subscribe up to £20,000 to an ISA in the tax year. For 2015/16 and 2016/17, the annual limit is £15,240. For 2014/15, the annual limit is £15,000 (but note that, before 1 July 2014, the annual limit was £11,880 of which a maximum of £5,940 could be saved in cash with one provider). For 2013/14 the overall limit is £11,520 and the cash limit is

£5,760; and for 2012/13 the limits are £11,289 and £5,640. See further details below. Cash ISAs can be opened by 16 and 17-year olds. There is no statutory lock-in, minimum subscription, minimum holding period or lifetime subscription limit. Withdrawals may be made at any time without loss of tax relief but not so as to allow further subscriptions in breach of the annual maximum.

Where an ISA investor dies on or after 3 December 2014, their surviving spouse or civil partner is given an additional ISA allowance equivalent to the value of the deceased spouse or partner's ISAs (other than junior ISAs). The deceased and the spouse or civil partner must have been living together at the time of death. The surviving spouse or civil partner can reinvest non-cash assets inherited by them which were included in the deceased's ISA. Non-cash assets must be reinvested within the period beginning with the distribution of the assets to the surviving spouse or civil partner or, if later, 6 April 2015 and ending 180 days later. Cash must be invested in the period beginning with the date of death or 6 April 2015 if later and ending three years later or, if later, 180 days after the administration of the estate is complete. With effect from 15 September 2016, the Treasury may make regulations to allow ISA-status for investments made before death to continue during the post-death administration period.

For 2016/17 onwards, the terms and conditions of an account may allow an investor to replace cash withdrawn from an ISA earlier in the year without the replacement counting towards the annual subscription limit for that year.

From 1 December 2015, the Government has introduced Help to Buy ISAs under which a bonus will be paid at the time savings are used to purchase a home. Lifetime ISAs have been introduced from 6 April 2017 for adults under the age of 40 under which a bonus will be paid at the time savings are used to purchase a home or on withdrawal of funds after age 60. Only one bonus from a Help to Buy or Lifetime ISA can be used to purchase a home.

Interest and dividends are free of income tax. With effect from 1 February 2016, where an amount is withdrawn from a Help to Buy ISA on the closure of that account, an equivalent amount may be invested in an ISA within 12 months without counting towards the annual limit if the house purchase falls through.

Gains arising from assets held within an ISA are not chargeable gains for CGT purposes (and losses are not allowable).

With effect from 1 November 2011 a 'junior ISA' is available for children who did not qualify for a child trust fund (see **25.24** above). Subscriptions of up to £4,128 (£4,080 before 6 April 2017; £3,840 before 1 July 2014; £3,720 before 6 April 2014; £3,600 before 6 April 2013) can be made in each tax year and can be saved in cash or stocks and shares. The funds are locked in until the child reaches adulthood. With effect from 6 April 2015, child trust funds can be transferred to junior ISAs without using up any of the annual limit for the year of transfer.

[*TCGA 1992, s 151; ITTOIA 2005, ss 694–701; FA 2011, s 40; FA 2016, s 27*].

The Individual Savings Account Regulations 1998 (SI 1998 No 1870 as amended) provide for the setting up of ISAs by HMRC-approved accounts managers, for the conditions under which they may invest and under which the accounts are to operate, for relief from tax in respect of account investments, and for general administration. The regulations are summarised below.'

Lifetime ISAs

A new section is added following the section headed 'Help to Buy ISAs' as follows.

'Lifetime ISAs are available from 6 April 2017. Accounts can be opened by individuals aged 18 or over but under 40 who are either resident in the UK or a Crown Servant. The maximum annual investment is £4,000 and investments can be made until the individual reaches 50. A government bonus of 25% of the amount invested (maximum £1,000) is added each tax year. Amounts invested in a Lifetime ISA count towards the investor's overall annual investment limit. Lifetime ISAs can hold cash, qualifying stocks and shares or a combination of both.

With effect from 6 April 2018, investors withdrawing amounts from a Lifetime ISA are liable to a 25% withdrawal charge. The charge does not apply if the investor is aged 60 or over, if the funds are used towards the purchase of a first home (value up to £450,000) or if the investor is terminally ill with less than 12 months to live. The account ends on death, with no withdrawal charge applying. Funds in a Lifetime ISA can only be used to purchase a first home if the account has been open for at least 12 months.

Holders of a Help to Buy ISA can transfer the savings into a Lifetime ISA in 2017/18 (without the amount counting towards the annual limit) or can continue to save into both. Only the government bonus from one of the accounts can be used in buying a first home.'

Tax exemptions

The text is replaced by the following.

'Except as stated below, no income tax or capital gains tax is chargeable on the account manager or the investor in respect of interest, dividends, distributions, gains, alternative financial arrangement return or building society bonus on ISA investments. Capital losses are not allowable.

Before 1 July 2014, interest on a cash deposit held within a stocks and shares component was, however, taxable at the basic rate of income tax, such tax to be accounted for by the account manager (by set-off against tax repayments or otherwise). There was no further liability; the interest did not form part of the investor's total income and the tax paid could not be repaid to the investor.

As regards ISAs, other than junior ISAs, held by children under 18 (see above), the exemption for interest on a cash account does not prevent the application of the settlements legislation of *ITTOIA 2005, s 629* (see Tolley's Income Tax under Settlements) whereby (subject to a *de minimis* limit) the income of an unmarried minor on capital provided by a parent is taxable as if it were the parent's income. Such income arising in an ISA is therefore taxable. The Government has indicated that this rule does not apply to junior ISAs.

Exempt income and gains do not have to be reported in the investor's personal tax return.'

Account managers

The text is replaced by the following.

'The regulations cover qualification as an account manager, HMRC approval and withdrawal thereof, appointment of UK tax representatives of non-UK account managers, account managers ceasing to act or to qualify, claims for tax relief and agreement of liabilities, annual returns of income and of information, annual and interim tax repayment claims, record-keeping, and information to be provided to investors.

[*Savings (Government Contributions) Act 2017, ss 1, 3, Sch 1; SI 1998 Nos 1870, 3174; SI 2006 No 3194; SI 2007 No 2119; SI 2008 Nos 704, 1934; SI 2009 No 1550; SI 2010 No 2957; SI 2011 No 1780; SI 2012 No 1871; SI 2014 Nos 654, 1450; SI 2015 Nos 869, 941, 1370; SI 2016 Nos 16, 364; SI 2017 No 186*].

Separate regulations modify existing tax legislation so far as it concerns individual savings account business of insurance companies. [*SI 1998 No 1871 as amended*].'

28

Government Securities

Exempt securities

[28.2] The text is amended to read as follows.

'Government securities (and certain public corporation securities guaranteed by the Treasury) are specified as exempt, as described in **28.1** above, by the Treasury in the form of a statutory instrument. In practice, all UK government securities charged on the National Loans Fund are so specified.

Any security which is a strip (within *FA 1942, s 47*) of a security which is a gilt specified as exempt is also itself a gilt specified for the purposes of the exemption. The Treasury are given powers to amend the legislation by regulations in connection with the introduction of gilt strips. [*TCGA 1992, s 288(8), Sch 9 Pt I; FA 1996, s 202*].

Those securities specified as exempt are listed in *TCGA 1992, Sch 9 Pt II* as supplemented by *SI 1993 No 950, SI 1994 No 2656, SI 1996 No 1031, SI 2001 No 1122, SI 2002 No 2849, SI 2004 No 438, SI 2005 No 276, SI 2006 Nos 184, 3170, SI 2008 No 1588, SI 2010 No 416, SI 2011 No 1295, SI 2012 No 1843, SI 2013 No 2983, SI 2014 No 1120, SI 2015 No 1790* and *SI 2017 No 10*. A list of the exempt securities has been made available on the gov.uk website (www.gov.uk/gilt-edged-securities-exempt-from-capital-gains-tax).'

29

Groups of Companies

A new section is added to read as follows.

'Change of a company's nature

[29.21A] If:

(a)   within any period of three years, a company becomes a member of a group of companies and there is (either earlier or later in that period, or at the same time) 'a major change in the nature or conduct of a trade or business' carried on by that company immediately before it became a member of that group; or

(b)   at any time the scale of the activities in a trade or business carried on by a company has become small or negligible, and before any considerable revival of the trade or business, that company becomes a member of a group of companies,

the trade or business carried on before that change, or which has become small or negligible, is disregarded for the purposes of **29.21**(c) above in relation to any time before the company became a member of the group in question.

'*A major change in the conduct of a trade or business*' includes a reference to a major change in services or facilities provided or a major change in customers or, in the case of a company with investment business, a major change in the nature of investments held. Regard will also be had to appropriate changes in other factors such as the location of the company's business premises, the identity of the company's suppliers, management or staff, the company's methods of manufacture, or the company's pricing or purchasing policies to the extent that these factors indicate that a major change has occurred. Efficiency changes and technological advancements would not in themselves indicate that a major change in the nature or conduct of a trade or business has occurred.

HMRC will compare any two points in three years which include the date of change of ownership of the company. This applies even if the change is the result of a gradual process which began outside the period of three years mentioned in (a) above. HMRC take note of both qualitative and quantitative issues as discussed in the cases *Willis v Peeters Picture Frames Ltd* CA (NI) 1982, 56 TC 436 and *Purchase v Tesco Stores Ltd* Ch D 1984, 58 TC 46 respectively (HMRC Statement of Practice 10/91).

Where the operation of the above provisions depends on circumstances or events at a time after the company becomes a member of any group of companies (but not more than three years after), an assessment to give effect to the provisions may be made within six years from that time or the latest such time.

[*TCGA 1992, Sch 7A para 8; FA 2016, s 55*].'

31

HMRC — Confidentiality of Information

Introduction

[31.1] The following paragraph is added at the end.

'HMRC were held to have breached their duty of confidentiality in *R (oao Ingenious Media Holding plc) v HMRC* SC, [2016] STC 2306.'

Publication of details of deliberate tax defaulters

[31.3] The last paragraph is amended to read as follows.

'With effect from 1 April 2017, the above applies also where a body corporate, a partnership or one or more of the trustees of a settlement has incurred a penalty under **52.8** PENALTIES in respect of a deliberate inaccuracy involving an offshore matter or an offshore transfer or a penalty under **52.3** PENALTIES in respect of a deliberate failure which involves an offshore matter or an offshore transfer. In this case the Commissioners may publish information in respect of any individual who controls the body corporate or partnership ('control' being construed as in *CTA 2010, s 1124*) or any individual who is a trustee of the settlement, where in either case the individual has obtained a tax advantage (as in *FA 2013, s 208* — see **4.3** ANTI-AVOIDANCE) as a result of the inaccuracy or failure. This applies regardless of the amount of potential lost revenue, and the let-out applies only if the penalty is reduced, by reason of *unprompted* disclosure, to the full extent permitted.

[FA 2009, s 94; FA 2016, s 164; SI 2017 No 261].'

32

HMRC Explanatory Publications

HMRC explanatory pamphlets

[32.1] The table of pamphlets is updated to read as follows.

SA/BK4	Self-Assessment — A General Guide to Keeping Records (June 2003).
SA/BK8	Self-Assessment — Your Guide (June 2004).
CTSA/ BK4	A General Guide to Corporation Tax Self-Assessment (October 2000).
COP 1	Putting things right when we make mistakes (June 2003).
COP 8	Specialist investigations (fraud and bespoke avoidance) (November 2016)

COP 9 (2014)	HMRC investigations where we suspect tax fraud (June 2014).
AO 1	The adjudicator's office for complaints about HMRC and Valuation Office Agency (August 2008)
C/FS	Complaints and putting things right (August 2014)
CC/FS1a	General information about compliance checks (November 2014)
CC/FS1b	General information about checks by Campaigns and Projects (January 2017)
CC/FS1c	General information about compliance checks into large businesses (November 2015)
CC/FS2	Compliance checks — information notices (May 2015)
CC/FS3	Compliance checks — visits by agreement or with advance notice (October 2015)
CC/FS4	Compliance checks — visits — unannounced (March 2009)
CC/FS5	Compliance checks — visits — unannounced — tribunal approved (March 2009)
CC/FS6	Compliance checks — what happens when we find something wrong (March 2009)
CC/FS7a	Compliance checks — penalties for inaccuracies in returns or documents (December 2016)
CC/FS7b	Compliance checks — penalties for not telling us about an under-assessment (November 2015)
CC/FS9	Compliance checks — Human Rights Act and penalties (November 2015)
CC/FS10	Compliance checks — suspending penalties for careless inaccuracies in returns or documents (December 2016)
CC/FS11	Compliance checks — penalties for failure to notify (November 2015)
CC/FS13	Compliance checks — publishing details of deliberate defaulters (November 2015)
CC/FS14	Compliance checks — managing serious defaulters (October 2015)
CC/FS15	Compliance checks — self assessment and old penalty rules (October 2015)
CC/FS17	Compliance checks — higher penalties for income tax and CGT involving offshore matters (October 2016)
CC/FS18(a)	Compliance checks — for failure to file annual and occasional returns and documents on time (December 2016)
CC/FS21	Compliance checks — alternative dispute resolution (October 2015)
CC/FS22	Compliance checks — sending electronic records to HMRC (October 2015)
CC/FS23	Compliance checks — third party information notices (May 2015)
CC/FS24	Tax avoidance schemes — accelerated payments (January 2017)

CC/FS25a	Tax avoidance schemes — follower notice and accelerated payments (except partnerships) (August 2016)
CC/FS25b	Tax avoidance schemes — partnership follower notice and accelerated partner payments (July 2016)
CC/FS30a	Compliance checks — tax avoidance schemes — penalties for follower notices (October 2016)
CC/FS30b	Compliance checks — tax avoidance schemes — penalties for partnership follower notices (March 2017)
CC/FS34	General anti-abuse rule and provisional counteraction notices (November 2016)
CC/FS38	Compliance checks — serial tax avoidance — warning notices (October 2016)
	Take care to avoid a penalty (July 2008)
HMRC 1	What to do if you disagree with HMRC decisions (January 2017)
Pride 1	Taxes and benefits — Information for our lesbian, gay, bisexual and transgender customers (download only — June 2009)
RDR1	Residence, Domicile and the Remittance Basis (September 2015)
RDR3	Statutory Residence Test (August 2016)
TH/FS1	Keeping records for business — what you need to know (February 2011)'

33

HMRC Extra-Statutory Concessions

The concessions

[33.2] The table of concessions is updated to read as follows.

'D2   **Residence in the UK: year of commencement or cessation of residence.** Subject to conditions based on previous residence status, split year treatment is available to an individual becoming or ceasing to be UK resident partway through a tax year. Superseded by the statutory residence test for 2013/14 onwards. See **57.29** RESIDENCE AND DOMICILE.

D3   **Private residence exemption: periods of absence (a).** Periods of absence are ignored where husband and wife are living together and the conditions are satisfied by the spouse who is not the owner. Superseded by statutory provision for disposals after 5 April 2009. See **53.7** PRIVATE RESIDENCES.

D4   **Private residence exemption: periods of absence (b).** Resumption of occupation after certain periods of absence will not be necessary if the terms of his employment require the taxpayer to work elsewhere. Superseded by statutory provision for disposals after 5 April 2009. See **53.7** PRIVATE RESIDENCES.

D6   **Private residence exemption: separated couples.** If, as the result of a breakdown of the marriage, one spouse ceases to occupy the matrimonial home and later transfers it (or part of it) as part of a financial settlement to the other spouse who has continued in occupation, no gain will be chargeable unless election has been made for some other house to be the main residence of the transferring spouse. Superseded by statutory provision for disposals after 5 April 2009. See **53.7** PRIVATE RESIDENCES.

D10   **Unquoted shares acquired before 6 April 1965: disposals following reorganisation of share capital.** Tax is not charged on a disposal of the entire new shareholding on more than the actual gains realised. See **8.10** ASSETS HELD ON 6 APRIL 1965.

D15   **Rollover relief: unincorporated associations.** Where property is held via the medium of a company in which at least 90% of the shares are held by the association or its members, the relief is available provided the other conditions are satisfied. Superseded by statutory provision for disposals after 5 April 2009. See **59.5** ROLLOVER RELIEF.

D16   **Rollover relief: repurchase of the same asset.** An asset which is repurchased for purely commercial reasons after having been sold may be treated as the 'new asset' for the purposes of the relief. See **59.2** ROLLOVER RELIEF.

D18   **Mortgage granted by vendor: subsequent default by purchaser as mortgagor.** In such circumstances and where the vendor regains beneficial ownership of the asset and so elects, the original sale is ignored and the chargeable gain arising is limited to the net proceeds obtained from the transactions. See **16.3** COMPUTATION OF GAINS AND LOSSES.

D21   **Private residence exemption: late elections in dual residence cases.** The two-year time limit will be extended in cases where the capital value of each of the residential interests, or each of them except one, is negligible and the individual was unaware of the possibility of electing. See **53.10** PRIVATE RESIDENCES.

D22   **Rollover relief: expenditure on improvements to existing assets.** Such expenditure is treated as incurred in acquiring other assets provided certain conditions are met. See **59.2** ROLLOVER RELIEF.

D23   **Rollover relief: partition of land and other assets on the dissolution of a partnership.** Partitioned assets are treated as 'new assets' for the purposes of the relief provided that the partnership is dissolved immediately thereafter. See **59.3** ROLLOVER RELIEF.

D24   **Rollover relief: assets not brought immediately into trading use.** The 'new asset' will qualify for relief even if not immediately taken into use for the purposes of the trade provided certain conditions are met. Land to be used for the site of a qualifying building will also qualify as the 'new asset' for the purposes of this concession subject to conditions. See **59.2** ROLLOVER RELIEF.

D25   **Rollover relief: acquisition of a further interest in an existing asset.** The further interest is treated as a 'new asset' for the purposes of the relief. See **59.2** ROLLOVER RELIEF.

D26   **Exchange of joint interests in land: form of rollover relief.** A form of rollover relief as on the compulsory purchase of land (see **41.12** LAND) is allowed on a disposal caused by the exchange of interests in land which is in the joint beneficial ownership of two or more persons. This relief is not confined to traders. The relief applies also to certain exchanges of milk or potato quota associated with such land. Superseded by statutory provision for disposals after 5 April 2010. See **41.13** LAND.

D32   **Transfer of a business to a company.** For the purposes of *TCGA 1992, s 162*, liabilities taken over by a company on the transfer are not treated as consideration so that no gain arises. See **37.2** INCORPORATION AND DISINCORPORATION RELIEFS.

D33   **Compensation and damages.** These are treated as derived from any underlying asset, and exempt or taxable accordingly, and as exempt if there is no underlying asset. See **7.2** ASSETS and **25.25** EXEMPTIONS AND RELIEFS.

D34   **Rebasing and indexation: shares held on 31 March 1982.** A single holding treatment will apply even if the shares were acquired on or before 6 April 1965. See **9.2** ASSETS HELD ON 31 MARCH 1982.

D35   **Employee trusts.** Concessional treatment will apply where an asset is transferred to a beneficiary who as a result suffers an income tax charge. Superseded by statutory provision for disposals after 5 April 2009. See **25.91** EXEMPTIONS AND RELIEFS.

D37   **Relocation of employees.** The exemption for a gain arising on the disposal of an employee's private residence is extended similarly to his right to share in any profits made by a relocation business or his employer to whom he sells property and which later sells it to a third party. Superseded by statutory provision for disposals after 5 April 2009. See **53.7** PRIVATE RESIDENCES.

D38   **Loans to traders evidenced by qualifying corporate bonds.** A further concessional relief will apply in certain circumstances where the bonds concerned only became qualifying corporate bonds because of a change in definition, even though they are not evidenced by a qualifying loan. Obsolete as regards loans made on or after 17 March 1998. See **44.14** LOSSES.

D39   **Extension of leases.** No capital gains tax is payable where a lessee surrenders an existing lease and is granted, in an arm's length transaction (or equivalent), a new, longer lease on the same property at a different rent, but otherwise on the same terms. See **41.15** LAND.

D40   **Non-resident trusts.** The definition of 'participator' in *ICTA 1988, s 417(1)* is concessionally restricted for the purposes of *TCGA 1992, s 96* and specified provisions of *TCGA 1992, Sch 5*. See **48.9, 48.19** OFFSHORE SETTLEMENTS.

D42   **Mergers of leases.** Where a superior interest in leasehold land is acquired (being either a superior lease or the reversion of freehold), and the land is disposed of after 28 June 1992, indexation allowance on the expenditure incurred on the inferior lease will be calculated by reference to the date of its acquisition. See **41.14** LAND.

D44   **Re-basing and indexation: shares derived from larger holdings held at 31 March 1982.** In certain circumstances a valuation of a shareholding held or treated as having been held at 31 March 1982 can be calculated by reference to the size of the shareholding held by a spouse or group member at that date. Superseded by statutory provision for disposals after 31 March 2010. See **9.6** ASSETS HELD ON 31 MARCH **1982.**

D45   **Rollover into depreciating assets.** Where an asset employed in a trade carried on by a claimant to rollover relief ceases to be used due to the claimant's death, no charge to tax will arise under *TCGA 1992, s 154(2)(b)*. Withdrawn with effect from 6 April 2016. See **59.9** ROLLOVER RELIEF.

D47   **Temporary loss of charitable status due to reverter of school and other sites.** A temporary loss of charitable status will in general be ignored for tax purposes. See **11.3** CHARITIES.

D49   **Private residence exemption: short delay by owner occupier in taking up residence.** Restriction of relief is removed in certain circumstances where an individual acquires a property but does not immediately use it as his only or main residence. See **53.7** PRIVATE RESIDENCES. This replaces SP D4.

D50   **Compensation for loss or deprivation of property situated outside the UK** does not give rise to a chargeable gain in specified circumstances. Concession superseded by statutory provision for compensation received after 5 April 2010 (31 March 2010 for corporation tax purposes). See **10.2** CAPITAL SUMS DERIVED FROM ASSETS.

D51   **Close company transferring asset at undervalue.** An anti-avoidance provision is not applied in two sets of circumstances. Superseded by statutory provision for disposals after 5 April 2009. See **4.14** ANTI-AVOIDANCE.

D52   **Share exchanges and company reconstructions: incidental costs of acquisition and disposal and warranty payments in respect of contingent liabilities.** Any such costs or payments are treated as allowable expenditure referable to the new holding of shares. See **63.5** and **63.7** SHARES AND SECURITIES.

D53   *TCGA 1992, s 50;* **Grants repaid.** Where a grant is repaid, and acquisition cost has been restricted by the amount of the grant, the consideration on disposal may be reduced by the amount repaid. See **16.13**(c) COMPUTATION OF GAINS AND LOSSES.

The following income tax and corporation tax concessions are also relevant for the purposes of capital gains tax or corporation tax on chargeable gains.

A11 **Residence in the UK: year of commencement or cessation of residence.** Although there is no provision for splitting a tax year in relation to residence, liability to UK tax which is affected by residence is computed by reference to the period of actual residence in the UK during the year. See also D2 above. Superseded by the statutory residence test for 2013/14 onwards. See Tolley's Income Tax.

A17 **Death of taxpayer before due date for payment of tax.** Personal representatives unable to pay tax before obtaining probate may have concessional treatment so that interest on tax falling due after the date of death runs from the later of the expiration of thirty days after the grant of probate and the statutory date for interest to run. Superseded by statutory provision for interest accruing on or after 31 October 2011. See **42.9** LATE PAYMENT INTEREST AND PENALTIES.

A19 **Arrears of tax arising through HMRC delay.** Arrears of tax arising due to the HMRC's failure to make proper and timely use of information supplied will be waived in certain cases. See **51.29** PAYMENT OF TAX.

A78 **Residence in the UK: accompanying spouse.** Where an employee leaving the UK to work abroad satisfies the conditions of A11 above, the residence treatment of the employee may be extended to an accompanying spouse in certain circumstances. Superseded by the statutory residence test for 2013/14 onwards. See **57.29–57.31** RESIDENCE AND DOMICILE.

A82 **Repayment supplement paid to individuals etc. resident in EC member states.** Residents of EC member states other than the UK will be treated on the same basis as UK residents in relation to a repayment supplement on a repayment of income tax. It is understood that this concession also applies to repayments of capital gains tax.

A94 **Profits and losses of theatre backers (angels).** Profits and losses of UK resident non-trading angels may be assessed and relieved as income. To be withdrawn with effect for all new productions from 1 April 2017. Productions using the concession before that date may continue to do so until 31 March 2019. See **44.9** LOSSES.

A99 **Tax treatment of compensation for mis-sold free standing additional voluntary contribution schemes.** Certain capital sums received by way of compensation are not regarded for capital gains tax purposes as the disposal of an asset. See **25.60** EXEMPTIONS AND RELIEFS.

B41 **Claims to repayment of tax.** Where an overpayment of tax arises because of an error by HMRC or another Government Department and where there is no dispute or doubt as to the facts, late claims to repayment of the tax overpaid will be allowed. See **51.29** PAYMENT OF TAX.

B46   **Late filing of company tax returns.** No flat-rate penalty will be charged if a return is received no later than the last business day within the seven days following the statutory filing date. See **52.4** PENALTIES.'

34

HMRC Investigatory Powers

Contractual disclosure facility

[34.13] The text is updated to read as follows.

'The contractual disclosure facility (CDF) commenced on 31 January 2012 is an opportunity offered to taxpayers to tell HMRC about any tax fraud in which they have been involved. See www.gov.uk/guidance/admitting-tax-fraud-the-contractual-disclosure-facility-cdf HMRC write to taxpayers whom they suspect have committed a tax fraud; their letter will offer a CDF contract and will be accompanied by a copy of COP 9 (see above). Taxpayers have 60 days from date of receipt to either accept or formally reject the offer of a contract. If they accept, they must produce an Outline Disclosure within the same 60-day period; this should contain a brief description of the frauds committed, a formal admission of deliberately bringing about a loss of tax, details of any non-fraudulent irregularities and any proposals for a payment on account. If the Outline Disclosure is accepted, the taxpayer will be required to make progress towards the production of a Certificate of Full Disclosure.

Under the terms of the CDF contract the taxpayer will not be criminally investigated, with a view to prosecution, for matters covered by the Outline Disclosure. The customer's co-operation will have the potential to maximise reductions in penalties. If the taxpayer rejects the offer of a contract or makes no response, HMRC have the option of starting a criminal investigation, though in most cases they will pursue a civil investigation.

See also HMRC Fraud Civil Investigation Manual FCIM101000 where the CDF contract is offered before 30 June 2014 and FCIM200000 where it is offered on or after that date.

If a taxpayer wishes to own up to a fraud without waiting to be contacted by HMRC, he may complete form CDF1 (www.gov.uk/government/publications/voluntary-disclosure-contractual-disclosure-facility-cdf1) or use the digital disclosure service (see below); HMRC will then consider the taxpayer for a CDF contract.

Digital disclosure service

Taxpayers wishing to disclose unreturned or unpaid taxes (including capital gains tax and corporation tax) may do so online using HMRC's digital disclosure service. Disclosures may be made under any of HMRC's campaigns or otherwise. See www.gov.uk/government/publications/hm-revenue-and-customs-disclosure-service.'

Data-gathering powers

[34.17] The following paragraph is added immediately before the heading 'Penalties' as follows.

'Money service businesses (i.e. businesses that provide money transfer, cheque cashing and currency exchange services), excluding banks, are to be added to the list.

Draft regulations are not expected to be introduced until Summer 2017, but will then have effect in relation to relevant data with a bearing on any period.

For details, see www.gov.uk/government/publications/data-from-money-servi ce-businesses.'

37

Incorporation and Disincorporation Reliefs

Transfer of business to a company — incorporation relief

[37.2] The last four paragraphs before the heading 'Interaction with other reliefs' are amended to read as follows.

'HMRC are prepared not to treat the assumption of business liabilities by the transferee company as consideration for the transfer; the relief is not precluded if some or all of the liabilities of the business are not taken over by the company. However, the assumption of *personal* liabilities, which includes tax liabilities pertaining to the unincorporated business, is treated as part of the consideration. (HMRC Extra-Statutory Concession D32 and see also HMRC Capital Gains Manual CG65745). (See **4.19** ANTI-AVOIDANCE for the charge arising where concessions involving deferral of gains are abused.)

If some of the assets are retained by the original owner, relief under *TCGA 1992, s 162* above is not available and liability to capital gains tax arises by reference to the market value of any chargeable assets transferred. Where *s 162* relief is not available, it is likely that a business asset hold-over relief claim under *TCGA 1992, s 165* (see **36.2** above) will prevail, provided that the transfer is by way of a non-arm's length bargain, including a transaction deemed to be such because it is between connected persons (see **4.12** ANTI-AVOIDANCE) (see HMRC Capital Gains Manual CG66973–66979).

Relief under *TCGA 1992, s 162* is available to individuals who are members of a partnership (even if one of the partners is a company) where the whole of the partnership business is transferred to a company. The relief is computed separately for each individual partner and is not precluded by virtue of any other partner receiving all or part of his consideration otherwise than in shares. HMRC consider that relief is not available where a partnership incorporates into an existing corporate partner. As the corporate partner already owns a share of the business assets, the whole of the business is not transferred (HMRC Capital Gains Manual CG65700).

For further commentary and examples, see HMRC Capital Gains Manual CG65700–65765.'

38

Indexation

Calculation of indexation allowance

[38.2] The final table of retail prices index factors is updated to read as follows.

	2012	2013	2014	2015	2016
Jan	238.0	245.8	252.6	255.4	258.80
Feb	239.9	247.6	254.2	256.7	260.00
Mar	240.8	248.7	254.8	257.1	261.1
Apr	242.5	249.5	255.7	258.0	261.4
May	242.4	250.0	255.9	258.5	262.1
Jun	241.8	249.7	256.3	258.9	263.1
Jul	242.1	249.7	256.0	258.6	263.4
Aug	243.0	251.0	257.0	259.8	264.4
Sep	244.2	251.9	257.6	259.6	264.9
Oct	245.6	251.9	257.7	259.5	264.8
Nov	245.6	252.1	257.1	259.8	265.5
Dec	246.8	253.4	257.5	260.6	267.1

Disposals on a no gain/no loss basis

[38.4] The text is amended to read as follows.

'On a 'no gain/no loss disposal' by a company, both the disposal consideration of the transferor and the corresponding acquisition consideration of the transferee are calculated for the purposes of *TCGA 1992* on the assumption that, on the disposal, an unindexed gain accrues to the transferor which is equal to the indexation allowance on that disposal, and so that after taking account of the indexation allowance the disposal is one on which neither a gain nor a loss accrues. This rule applied also to such disposals by individuals, trustees or personal representatives before 6 April 2008. Where the acquisition consideration for an asset was determined in this way, the amount of that consideration is not affected by the abolition of indexation allowance for capital gains tax purposes.

For the purposes of calculating indexation allowance under *TCGA 1992, ss 53, 54* (see 38.2 above), any enactment is disregarded to the extent to which it provides that, on a subsequent disposal of an asset by the transferee which was acquired by him on a no gain/no loss disposal as above, the transferor's acquisition of the asset is to be treated as the transferee's acquisition of it. [*TCGA 1992, ss 52A, 56(2)*]. For further applications of this provision, see **9.6** ASSETS HELD ON 31 MARCH **1982** and **64.4** SHARES AND SECURITIES — IDENTIFICATION RULES.

Where otherwise a loss would accrue on the disposal of an asset, and the sums allowable as a deduction in computing the loss would include an amount attributable to the application of the assumption contained in *TCGA 1992, s 56(2)* above on any no gain/no loss disposal, those sums are determined as if *TCGA 1992, s 56(2)* had not applied and the loss is reduced accordingly or, if those sums are then equal to or less than the consideration for the disposal, the disposal is to be one on which neither a gain nor a loss accrues. [*TCGA 1992, s 56(3)*].

For the purposes of *TCGA 1992, s 56(1)* (part disposals; see **38.3** above) and *TCGA 1992, s 56(2)(3)* above, a '*no gain/no loss disposal*' is one which, by virtue of any enactment other than *TCGA 1992, s 35(4)* (no gain/no loss disposal where the general re-basing rule of *TCGA 1992, s 35(1)(2)* would otherwise convert a gain into a loss and vice versa; see **9.2** ASSETS HELD ON 31 MARCH **1982**), *s 53(1)* (no gain/no loss disposal where indexation allowance equals or exceeds gain before indexation; see **38.2** above) or *s 56* itself, is treated as a disposal on which neither a gain nor a loss accrues. [*TCGA 1992, s 56(4)*]. For these purposes the definition is not therefore confined to those no gain/ no loss disposals mentioned in **9.6** ASSETS HELD ON 31 MARCH **1982**.'

Options

[38.8] The first paragraph is amended to read as follows.

'Where, on a disposal, relevant allowable expenditure includes both:

(a) the cost of acquiring an option binding the grantor to sell ('*the option consideration*'); and
(b) the cost of acquiring what was sold as a result of the exercise of the option ('*the sale consideration*'),

the option consideration and sale consideration are regarded as separate items of expenditure incurred when the option was acquired and when the sale took place respectively. An option binding the grantor both to sell and to buy is treated for these purposes as two separate options with one half of the consideration attributable to each. These provisions do not apply where those at **64.4** SHARES AND SECURITIES — IDENTIFICATION RULES (under 'Consideration for options') apply. [*TCGA 1992, s 145*].'

42

Late Payment Interest and Penalties

Late payment interest (the new regime)

[42.2] The table of rates of interest is updated to read as follows.

'Rates of interest are:

2.75% p.a. from 23 August 2016
3.00% p.a. from 31 October 2011 to 22 August 2016'

Companies

[42.7] The table of rates of interest is updated to read as follows.

'The rates of interest (such interest being deductible for tax purposes — see below) as regards corporation tax becoming due **on or after the normal due date** (nine months and one day after the end of the accounting period) are:

2.75% p.a. from 23 August 2016
3.00% p.a. from 29 September 2009 to 22 August 2016
2.50% p.a. from 24 March 2009 to 28 September 2009
3.50% p.a. from 27 January 2009 to 23 March 2009
4.50% p.a. from 6 January 2009 to 26 January 2009
5.50% p.a. from 6 December 2008 to 5 January 2009
6.50% p.a. from 6 November 2008 to 5 December 2008
7.50% p.a. from 6 January 2008 to 5 November 2008
8.50% p.a. from 6 August 2007 to 5 January 2008
7.50% p.a. from 6 September 2006 to 5 August 2007
6.50% p.a. from 6 September 2005 to 5 September 2006
7.50% p.a. from 6 September 2004 to 5 September 2005
6.50% p.a. from 6 December 2003 to 5 September 2004
5.50% p.a. from 6 August 2003 to 5 December 2003
6.50% p.a. from 6 November 2001 to 5 August 2003
7.50% p.a. from 6 May 2001 to 5 November 2001
8.50% p.a. previously

The rates for corporation tax payable by earlier **instalments,** under the quarterly accounting rules for large companies (see **51.4** PAYMENT OF TAX), are:

1.25% p.a. from 15 August 2016
1.50% p.a. from 16 March 2009 to 14 August 2016
2.00% p.a. from 16 February 2009 to 15 March 2009
2.50% p.a. from 19 January 2009 to 15 February 2009
3.00% p.a. from 15 December 2008 to 18 January 2009
4.00% p.a. from 17 November 2008 to 14 December 2008
5.50% p.a. from 20 October 2008 to 16 November 2008
6.00% p.a. from 21 April 2008 to 19 October 2008
6.25% p.a. from 18 February 2008 to 20 April 2008
6.50% p.a. from 17 December 2007 to 17 February 2008
6.75% p.a. from 16 July 2007 to 16 December 2007
6.50% p.a. from 21 May 2007 to 15 July 2007
6.25% p.a. from 22 January 2007 to 20 May 2007
6.00% p.a. from 20 November 2006 to 21 January 2007
5.75% p.a. from 14 August 2006 to 19 November 2006
5.50% p.a. from 15 August 2005 to 13 August 2006
5.75% p.a. from 16 August 2004 to 14 August 2005
5.50% p.a. from 21 June 2004 to 15 August 2004
5.25% p.a. from 17 May 2004 to 20 June 2004
5.00% p.a. from 16 February 2004 to 16 May 2004

4.75% from 17 November 2003 to 15 February 2004
4.50% p.a. from 21 July 2003 to 16 November 2003
4.75% p.a. from 17 February 2003 to 20 July 2003
5.00% p.a. from 19 November 2001 to 16 February 2003
5.50% p.a. from 15 October 2001 to 18 November 2001
5.75% p.a. from 1 October 2001 to 14 October 2001
6.00% p.a. from 13 August 2001 to 30 September 2001
6.25% p.a. from 21 May 2001 to 12 August 2001
6.50% p.a. from 16 April 2001 to 20 May 2001
6.75% p.a. from 19 February 2001 to 15 April 2001
7.00% p.a. from 20 April 2000 to 18 February 2001
8.00% p.a. from 21 February 2000 to 19 April 2000
7.75% p.a. from 24 January 2000 to 20 February 2000
7.50% p.a. from 15 November 1999 to 23 January 2000
7.25% p.a. from 20 September 1999 to 14 November 1999
7.00% p.a. from 21 June 1999 to 19 September 1999
7.25% p.a. from 19 April 1999 to 20 June 1999
7.50% p.a. from 15 February 1999 to 18 April 1999
8.00% p.a. from 18 January 1999 to 14 February 1999
8.25% p.a. from 7 January 1999 to 17 January 1999'

44

Losses

Profit and losses of theatre backers (angels)

[44.9] The first paragraph is amended to read as follows.

'*Angels* are theatrical backers who invest in productions. An investment which occurs in the normal course of a backer's trade falls within the trading income rules (see Tolley's Income Tax). Special tax treatment applies to non-trading backers.'

The following paragraph is added at the end.

'The concession is to be withdrawn with effect for all new productions from 1 April 2017. Productions using the concession before that date may continue to do so until 31 March 2019. See www.gov.uk/government/publications/wit hdrawal-of-extra-statutory-concession-esc-a94-theatre-angels.'

Assets of negligible value

[44.11] The sixth paragraph is amended to read as follows.

'In *Director v Inspector of Taxes* (Sp C 161), [1998] SSCD 172, a negligible value claim was refused on the grounds that the shares in question had a nil acquisition cost by virtue of *TCGA 1992, s 17* (see **45.1** MARKET VALUE) and thus could not *become* of negligible value (but see (b) above). See also *Barker and others v HMRC* FTT 2011, [2012] SFTD 244 and *Dyer v HMRC* UT 2016, [2017] STC 189.'

Losses on shares in unlisted trading companies — individuals

[44.15] The following paragraph is added immediately before the heading 'Operation of and claims for relief'.

'In *Murray-Hession v HMRC FTT*, [2016] UKFTT 612 (TC) the taxpayer was held to have subscribed for shares previously held by another person as nominee, agent or otherwise on his behalf.'

49

Overseas Matters

UK resident participator in overseas resident company

[49.7] The paragraph immediately before the heading 'Exclusions' is amended to read as follows.

'References to a person's interest as a participator in a company are references to the interest in the company which is represented by all the factors by reference to which he falls to be treated as such a participator. References to the extent of such an interest are references to the proportion of the interests as participators of all the participators in the company (including any who are not resident or, for 2012/13 and earlier years, ordinarily resident in the UK) which on a just and reasonable apportionment is represented by that interest.'

The paragraph headed 'Losses' is updated to read as follows.

'Any loss arising on the disposal of assets by a non-resident company which would be a close company if it were UK resident can be similarly treated as accruing to the participator concerned, but only insofar as it reduces or extinguishes gains apportioned to him under these provisions and treated as accruing in the same year of assessment. Losses can be set off against gains of the same company or different companies (HMRC Capital Gains Manual CG57295).'

Tax collection agreement with Switzerland

[49.22] The text is replaced by the following.

'The UK Government entered into an agreement with Switzerland under which Swiss bank accounts of UK taxpayers were subject to a one-off deduction to settle unpaid UK tax liabilities and are subject to a withholding tax to satisfy ongoing liabilities. The legislation giving effect to the agreement (and subsequent amendments to it) in the UK is at *FA 2012, s 218, Sch 36*. The agreement took effect on 1 January 2013. The agreement is terminated on the coming into force of the automatic exchange of information agreement between Switzerland and the EU. That agreement provides for the exchange of account date from 2018.

Initial deduction

The initial deduction of between 21% and 41% of the funds in accounts held by individual UK taxpayers was taken from accounts in 2013 where the account was open on both 31 December 2010 and 31 May 2013. The deduction settled income tax, capital gains tax, inheritance tax and VAT liabilities in relation to the funds in the account. No deduction was applied if the taxpayer instructed the bank to disclose details of the account to HMRC. The effect was, in most cases, that amounts which suffered the deduction and on which the taxpayer should have paid tax, but which were untaxed, ceased to be liable to UK tax. In certain cases, however, the deduction was instead treated as a credit against UK tax, interest and penalties on the untaxed amount. Where the UK liability was removed, there are provisions to ensure that the taxpayer's liability to tax on other income or gains was what it would have been if the amounts no longer liable to UK tax had remained so liable. See *FA 2012, Sch 36 paras 2–12*.

Withholding tax

The withholding tax is applied from 2013 to income and gains arising on investments held by individual UK taxpayers in Swiss banks, the rates being close to the highest UK rates. For capital gains (as defined in the agreement), the rate is usually 27% (28% in certain cases). As with the initial deduction, the withholding tax does not apply if the taxpayer authorises the bank to disclose details to HMRC and pays any associated taxes in the UK. The effect of the withholding tax is that the taxpayer ceases to be liable to income tax or capital gains tax on the income or gain concerned, but the taxpayer can elect for the tax to be treated as a credit against income tax and/or capital gains tax. An election must be made in the tax return for the year concerned, and that return must include all of the income or gains in respect of which tax has been withheld. See *FA 2012, Sch 36 paras 13–19*.

Remittance basis

Where the taxpayer uses the remittance basis (55), foreign income or gains are treated as not remitted to the UK when money is brought to the UK pursuant to a transfer to HMRC in accordance with the agreement. If the money is transferred from a mixed fund, the bringing of it to the UK is treated as an offshore transfer (see 55.3 REMITTANCE BASIS). [*FA 2012, Sch 36 paras 26A, 26B; FA 2013, s 221*].'

52

Penalties

Introduction to penalties

[52.1] The section is updated to read as follows.

'Financial penalties can be charged or sought by HMRC for a substantial number of offences by taxpayers or their agents. The current penalties relevant to capital gains tax and corporation tax on chargeable gains are summarised in the table below and are described in detail in the paragraphs of this chapter or where indicated in the table.

Offence	Penalty		Para
1. Failure to notify charge-ability to tax. Failure to comply with the obligation to notify chargeability to CGT within six months of tax year or to CT within one year of accounting period. *FA 2008, Sch 41.*	Deliberate and concealed failure: 100% of potential lost revenue. Deliberate but unconcealed failure: 70% of potential lost revenue. Any other case: 30% of potential lost revenue. A statutory reduction in the amount of the penalty is made for disclosure of a failure. HMRC can also reduce a penalty in special circumstances. Where the failure is linked to an offshore matter relating to certain categorised territories the amount of the penalty is increased by 50% or 100%.		52.3
2. Failure to deliver corporation tax return on time. *TMA 1970, s 7; FA 1998, Sch 18 paras 17, 18.*	(i)	£100 if up to 3 months late (£500 if previous two returns also delivered late);	52.4
	(ii)	£200 if over 3 months late (£1,000 if previous two returns also late);	
Failure continuing at later of final day for delivery of return and 18 months after return period		Further penalty of 10% of tax unpaid 18 months after return period (20% of tax unpaid at that date if return not made within 2 years of return period)	
3. Failure to make return on time (income tax and capital gains tax). *FA 2009, Sch 55*	(i)	initial penalty of £100.	52.5
	(ii)	if failure continues three months after penalty date and HMRC give notice, a further penalty of £10 per day for each day failure continues in 90-day period beginning with date specified in notice.	
	(iii)	if failure continues six months after penalty date, a further penalty of the greater of 5% of the tax liability and £300.	

Offence		Penalty	Para
To be extended to corporation tax returns from a date to be fixed.	(iv)	if failure continues twelve months after penalty date and the withholding of information is deliberate or concealed a further penalty of the greater of 100% of the tax liability and £300; if the withholding is deliberate and not concealed, the greater of 70% of the liability and £300; or otherwise, greater of 5% of the liability and £300.	
		A statutory reduction in the amount of the penalty is made for disclosure of a failure. HMRC can also reduce a penalty in special circumstances. Where the failure is linked to an offshore matter relating to certain categorised territories the amount of the penalty is increased by 50% or 100%.	
4. **Failure to make payment of CGT on time.** *FA 2009, Sch 56*		A 5% penalty applies if full amount not paid within 30 days of due date. If amount remains unpaid six months after due date a penalty of 5% applies; a further 5% penalty applies if amount is still unpaid after a further six months.	42.10 LATE PAYMENT INTEREST AND PENALTIES
5. **Error in taxpayer's document.** Careless or deliberate error in document amounting to or leading to understatement of liability, overstatement or loss or false or inflated claim to repayment of tax. *FA 2007, Sch 24 para 1.*		Deliberate and concealed error: 100% of potential lost revenue. Deliberate but unconcealed error: 70% of potential lost revenue. Any other case: 30% of potential lost revenue. A statutory reduction in the amount of the penalty is made for disclosure of an error. HMRC can also reduce a penalty in special circumstances. Where the error is linked to an offshore matter relating to certain categorised territories the amount of the penalty is increased by 50% or 100%.	52.8

Offence	Penalty	Para
6. Error in taxpayer's document attributable to another person. Deliberately supplying false information to, or deliberately withholding information from, a person giving a document to HMRC resulting in document containing an inaccuracy amounting to or leading to understatement of liability, overstatement of loss or false or inflated claim to repayment of tax. *FA 2007, Sch 24 para 1A.*	100% of potential lost revenue subject to statutory reduction for disclosure or in special circumstances.	52.9
7. Failure to notify HMRC of error in assessment. Failure to take reasonable steps to notify HMRC of an under-assessment within the 30 days beginning with the date of the assessment. *FA 2007, Sch 24 para 2.*	30% of potential lost revenue subject to statutory reduction for disclosure or in special circumstances.	52.10
8. Arrangements counteracted under the GAAR. A person is liable to a penalty if HMRC counteract a tax advantage by making adjustments under the general anti-abuse rule ('GAAR'). *FA 2013, s 212A.*	60% of the counteracted advantage.	52.11
9. Offshore asset move where taxpayer becomes liable to another penalty under 1, 3 or 5 above. *FA 2015, Sch 21.*	50% of original penalty.	52.12
10. Asset-based penalty for offshore inaccuracies and failures. *FA 2016, Sch 22.*	Lower of (i) 10% of value of the asset, and (ii) the offshore potential lost revenue x 10.	52.13
11. Failure to maintain records. Failure to keep and preserve appropriate records supporting personal and trustees' returns or partnership returns. *TMA 1970, s 12B.*	Up to £3,000	52.14

Offence	Penalty		Para
12. **Failure to comply with HMRC investigatory powers.** Failure to comply with an information notice within *FA 2008, Sch 36 Pt 1* or deliberately obstructing an HMRC officer in the course of an inspection of business premises under *FA 2008, Sch 36 Pt 2* which has been approved by the First-tier Tribunal. *FA 2008, Sch 36.*	(i)	initial penalty of £300.	**52.16**
	(ii)	if failure/obstruction continues, a further penalty up to £60 per day.	
	(iii)	if failure/obstruction continues after penalty under (i) imposed, a tax-related amount determined by the Upper Tribunal.	
13. **HMRC investigatory powers: inaccurate information and documents** *FA 2008, Sch 36.*	Up to £3,000		**52.16**
14. **HMRC data-gathering powers: failure to comply** *FA 2011, Sch 23.*	(i)	initial penalty of £300.	**52.17**
	(ii)	if failure continues, a further penalty up to £60 per day.	
	(iii)	if failure continues for more than 30 days after penalty under (ii) imposed, a further daily penalty determined by the Upper Tribunal up to £1,000 per day.	
15. **HMRC data-gathering powers: inaccurate data** *FA 2011, Sch 23.*	Up to £3,000		**52.17**
16. **Dishonest conduct by tax agents** *FA 2012, Sch 38 para 26.*	Up to £50,000 (minimum £5,000)		**52.19**
17. **Tax agents: failure to comply with file access notice** *FA 2012, Sch 38 paras 22, 23.*	(i)	Initial penalty of £300.	
	(ii)	If failure continues, a further penalty up to £60 per day.	**52.19**
18. **Enabling offshore tax evasion** *FA 2016, s 162, Sch 20*	Higher of 100% of the potential lost revenue and £3,000. If the original tax non-compliance resulted in a penalty under *FA 2015, Sch 21* (see 9 above), higher of 50% of the potential lost revenue in respect of the original tax non-compliance and £3,000.		**52.20**

Offence	Penalty		Para
19. Special returns etc. Failure to comply with a notice to deliver any return or other document, to furnish any particulars, to produce any document or record, to make anything available for inspection or give any certificate under specified provisions. *TMA 1970, s 98.*	Up to £300 (£3,000 in specified cases)		52.23
20. Failure to disclose tax avoidance scheme. Failure to comply with any of a number of requirements under the disclosure of tax avoidance schemes rules. *TMA 1970, s 98C.*	(i)	Initial penalty of £5,000.	52.24
	(ii)	continuing daily penalty of £600 (£5,000 in specified cases) after penalty in (i) has been imposed.	
	(iii)	Penalty of £100 for failure of party to notifiable arrangements to notify HMRC of scheme reference number. Increased to £500 for second failure in three-year period and £1,000 for third failure.	
21. High-risk promoters of avoidance schemes. Failure to comply with any of a number of requirements under the high-risk promoters of avoidance schemes rules. Provision of inaccurate information or documents in compliance with such a requirement. *FA 2014, Sch 35.*	Various		52.25
22. Failure to comply with a follower notice. [*FA 2014, s 208*].	Up to 50% of the value of the denied tax advantage or 20% in partnership cases.		52.26
23. Failure to make accelerated payment. [*FA 2014, s 226*].	A 5% penalty applies if full amount not paid by due date. If amount remains unpaid five months after due date a penalty of 5% applies; a further 5% penalty applies if amount is still unpaid after a further six months.		52.27

Offence	Penalty		Para
24. Powers of enforcement by deduction from accounts. [F(No 2)A 2015, Sch 8]. Various compliance failures or making disclosure likely to prejudice HMRC's ability to use the powers to recover the sum in question.	(i)	Initial penalty of £300.	52.28
	(ii)	If failure continues, a further penalty up to £60 per day.	
25. Penalties under the serial avoiders regime. [FA 2016, Sch 18]. Where a person suffers a defeat of an avoidance scheme used whilst in a warning period.	Penalty of 20% of the value of the counteracted advantage. If, before the relevant defeat is incurred, the person was liable to be given prior warning notices, the penalty is increased. It is increased to 40% where there has been a single prior warning notice, and to 60% where there has been more than one such notice.		52.29
26. Failure to comply with requirement to publish tax strategy. [FA 2016, Sch 19].	(i)	Initial penalty of £7,500.	52.30
	(ii)	If failure continues for six months, a further penalty of £7,500.	
	(iii)	If failure continues, a further penalty of £7,500 at the end of each subsequent month.	

Superseded penalties which are still relevant to the last five years are also described in this chapter. See **52.21** below.

For the procedure for charging penalties see **52.33** onwards below. See **52.40** below for potential liability under the criminal law.

Failure to correct past offshore evasion

HMRC is consulting until 19 October 2016 on a proposed new set of penalties for failure to disclose undeclared UK tax liabilities in respect of an offshore matter by September 2018. See HMRC Notice 24 August 2016. Increased penalties are likely to apply where a taxpayer fails to take advantage of HMRC's worldwide disclosure facility which opened on 5 September 2016, for which see HMRC Notice 25 August 2016.

Enablers of tax avoidance

Following consultation conducted earlier in 2016, a new penalty will be introduced in Finance Bill 2017. The penalty will apply to individuals or entities ('enablers') who enable the use of abusive tax arrangements which HMRC later defeat. It will apply only to steps taken by enablers after Royal Assent to Finance Bill 2017.

The definition of 'enabler' will distinguish between those who design, market or otherwise facilitate avoidance arrangements and those who just advise, report or otherwise provide an opinion on such arrangements and whose advice does not result in any changes to the arrangements. Anyone unwittingly becoming involved in arrangements will be excluded.

Arrangements will be treated as abusive if they meet a 'double reasonableness test'. This will ensure that the penalty does not inhibit genuine commercial transactions. External scrutiny will be provided by the GAAR Advisory Panel.

The penalty will apply to arrangements relating to income tax, corporation tax, CGT, petroleum revenue tax, diverted profits tax, apprenticeship levy, inheritance tax, SDLT or annual tax on enveloped dwellings.

The amount of the penalty will be equal to the consideration received by the enabler for anything done to enable the arrangements. HMRC will be able to publish information about an enabler liable to penalties exceeding a specified amount (yet to be fixed).

See www.gov.uk/government/publications/strengthening-sanctions-and-deterrents-for-tax-avoidance.

Reasonable care

The circumstances in which a taxpayer is considered to have taken reasonable care for the purposes of the penalty provisions of *FA 2007, Sch 24* (see **52.8** below) are to be amended. The changes will apply to documents relating to tax periods which begin on or after 6 April 2017 and end on or after the date of Royal Assent to Finance Bill 2017.

Following the changes it will be presumed in cases of defeated avoidance that a person has been careless unless they can prove they have taken reasonable care. The legislation will explicitly describe circumstances and events which do not represent taking reasonable care. These will include:

(a)   advice addressed to a third party or without reference to the tax-payer's specific circumstances and use of the scheme;

(b)   advice commissioned or funded by a party with a direct financial interest in selling the scheme or not provided by a disinterested party; and

(c)   material produced by parties without the relevant tax or legal expertise or experience to advise on complicated avoidance arrangements (typically the sort of material used to market arrangements and not amounting to advice on the legal options necessary for a taxpayer to assess the likely success of the scheme or the risks).

See www.gov.uk/government/publications/strengthening-sanctions-and-deterrents-for-tax-avoidance.

Requirement to correct

Legislation in Finance Bill 2017 will introduce a new requirement for those who have failed to declare UK tax on offshore interests to correct that situation by disclosing the relevant information to HMRC. This new requirement to correct (RTC) will apply to all taxpayers with offshore interests who have not complied with their UK tax obligations.

Taxpayers who have 'relevant offshore tax non-compliance' at 5 April 2017, and who fail to correct it within the RTC period (see below), will be liable to a penalty. The provisions apply to the following failures in relation to income tax, capital gains tax (and inheritance tax) which involve offshore matters:

(a) failure to notify chargeability to tax;

(b) failure to make and deliver a return; and

(c) delivering an inaccurate document (for example, a return) to HMRC.

The maximum penalty for failure to correct (FTC) is 200% of the potential lost revenue relating to the relevant offshore tax non-compliance that has not been corrected within the RTC period. HMRC may reduce the penalty to reflect the quality of the taxpayer's disclosure, but not below 100% of the potential lost revenue. The following additional penalties may be charged:

(i) an asset-based penalty of up to 10% of the value of the relevant asset in the most serious cases; and

(ii) an enhanced penalty of 50% of the amount of the standard penalty, if HMRC can show that assets or funds have been moved to attempt to avoid the requirement to correct.

HMRC may publish information about a person who incurs one or more FTC penalties involving potential lost revenue exceeding £25,000, or if the person incurs five or more FTC penalties.

The RTC measure will have effect after Royal Assent to the Finance Bill 2017, the RTC window for correction to be made will run from the date of Royal Assent to the Finance Act 2017 to 30 September 2018, and from 1 October 2018 a penalty will apply to those who have failed to correct before 30 September 2018.

For details, see www.gov.uk/government/publications/tackling-offshore-tax-ev asion-requirement-to-correct.'

Cross-tax penalty for failure to make returns

[52.5] The following paragraph is added immediately before the heading 'Reduction for disclosure'.

'In *Chartridge Developments Ltd v HMRC* FTT 2016, [2017] UKFTT 766 (TC), 2017 STI 332, the taxpayer had delegated the task of submitting a return to an employee who had failed to do so. The company was held not to have a reasonable excuse as there was no evidence that it had taken any steps to ensure that the return would be submitted on time or to check that it had in fact been submitted other than delegating the task to the employee.'

Penalty for offshore asset moves

[52.12] The first paragraph is amended to read as follows.

'With effect for movements occurring after 26 March 2015, a penalty (the '*offshore asset moves penalty*') applies where assets are moved between overseas territories and a main purpose of that movement is to prevent or delay the discovery by HMRC of a potential loss of revenue that itself gives rise to one of the pre-existing penalties mentioned below. The offshore asset moves penalty is intended to address a risk that assets will be moved from territories committed to exchanging information under the Organisation for Economic Co-operation and Development's Common Reporting Standard to other territories for the purpose of continuing to conceal past failures or actions for which pre-existing penalties are chargeable.'

Asset-based penalty for offshore inaccuracies and failures

[52.13] The first paragraph is amended to read as follows.

'An asset-based penalty is payable by a person where:

(a)   one or more 'offshore tax penalties' have been imposed on a person in relation to 2016/17 or a subsequent tax year; and

(b)   the potential lost revenue threshold is met in relation to that year.'

The last paragraph under the heading 'Identification and valuation of assets' is amended to read as follows.

'Where an asset-based penalty is chargeable in relation to an asset that is jointly held by the taxpayer (P) and another person (A), the value of the asset is the value of P's share of it. If P and A are living together in a marriage or civil partnership, the asset is taken to be jointly owned by them in equal shares, unless it appears to HMRC that this is not the case.

[FA 2016, s 165, Sch 22 paras 1–11, 14, 19; SI 2017 No 277].'

Failure to produce documents during enquiry

[52.15] The section is deleted.

Enabling offshore tax evasion

[52.20] The first paragraph is amended to read as follows.

'With effect for acts or omissions occurring on or after 1 January 2017, a penalty is payable by a person (P) who has 'enabled' another person (Q) to carry out offshore tax evasion or non-compliance if:

(a)   P knew when his actions were carried out that they enabled, or were likely to enable, Q to carry out such evasion or non-compliance; and

(b)   either:

(i)   Q has been convicted of one of the offences listed below and the conviction is final; or

(ii)   Q has been found to be liable to one of the penalties listed below and either the penalty is final or a contract settlement with HMRC has been agreed under which HMRC undertake not to assess the penalty or to take proceedings to recover it.'

The paragraph under the heading 'Double jeopardy' is amended to read as follows.

'A person is not liable to a penalty under these provisions in respect of conduct for which he has been convicted of an offence or has been assessed to another penalty.

[*FA 2016, s 162, Sch 20 paras 1–9, 15; SI 2016 No 1249*].'

55
Remittance Basis

Introduction to the remittance basis

[55.1] The following text is added after the fourth paragraph.

'**2017/18 onwards**

From 6 April 2017, an individual will be deemed domiciled in the UK for the purposes of income tax and capital gains tax if he:

(a)   was born in the UK with a UK domicile of origin and is UK resident in the tax year (i.e. he is non-domiciled under general law having acquired a foreign domicile of choice); or

(b)   has been resident in the UK for at least 15 out of the last 20 tax years (although this condition does not apply if the individual is non-resident from 6 April 2017 onwards).

The individual who is deemed domicile under condition (b) above who wishes to reset the clock for deemed domicile purposes must be non-resident for six complete tax years before returning to the UK.

The £90,000 remittance basis charge for those who have been UK resident for at least 17 out of the last 20 years will be repealed as those individuals cannot access the remittance basis.

The deemed domicile rules will not apply to any individual whose unremitted foreign income and gains is less than £2,000 in the tax year. These individuals can continue to use the remittance basis automatically in 2017/18 and subsequent years.

The irrevocable capital loss election which non-domiciles can make under *TCGA 1992, ss 16ZA–16ZC* (see **55.2** below) will fall away once the individual becomes deemed UK-domiciled. All UK deemed domiciles will be able to utilise foreign capital losses arising during the period of deemed domicile under the normal capital loss rules.

Transitional rules will apply for the temporary non-residence rules for capital gains tax. The new deemed domicile rules can be ignored for determining the UK capital gains tax under the temporary non-residence rules so long as the period of non-residence is deemed to begin before 8 July 2015.

Capital gains rebasing

Any individual who is treated as deemed domiciled under the new 15-year test in 2017/18 can rebase their foreign chargeable assets to their market value on 5 April 2017. To qualify the individual must have paid the remittance basis charge at some point and be deemed UK-domiciled under the 15-year rule in the tax year in which the disposal occurs.'

The final paragraph is amended to read as follows.

'This does not apply to those who first meet the 15-year in a tax year later than 2017/18 and does not apply to those who meet the other condition for deemed domicile (i.e. those born in the UK with a UK domicile of origin who return to the UK).'

The following text is added at the end.

'Cleansing of mixed funds

There is to be a one-off opportunity to separate mixed funds into their constituent parts for those individuals who are:

(a)   non-domiciled under general law (so long as they were not born in the UK with a UK domicile of origin); and
(b)   have used the remittance basis (either automatically or by making a claim) at any tax year prior to 2017/18.

It does not matter whether or not the individual is caught by the new deemed domicile rules. No funds should be separated until after 6 April 2017 and this exercise should be completed by 5 April 2019.

See www.gov.uk/government/publications/income-tax-inheritance-tax-and-ca pital-gains-tax-deemed-domicile-rule.'

58

Returns

Introduction to returns

[58.1] The fourth paragraph is replaced by the following.

Making tax digital

'The Government intends to abolish tax returns for income tax and capital gains tax and replace them with digital tax accounts. Individuals will be given access to their digital tax accounts in 2016 with returns being phased out by 2021. On 15 August 2016, HMRC published six consultation documents covering various aspects of the proposed changes. On 31 January 2017, they published responses to the consultation documents together with draft legislation for the Finance Bill 2017. The draft legislation relates to the core compliance rules and business profits. See generally www.gov.uk/governmen t/publications/making-tax-digital.'

Completion of enquiry

[58.12] The text is replaced by the following.

'An enquiry is completed when an HMRC officer gives the taxpayer notice (closure notice) that he has completed his enquiries and states his conclusions. The closure notice takes effect when it is issued and must either make the necessary amendments to the return to give effect to the stated conclusions or state that no amendment of the return is required. Before the enquiry is complete, the taxpayer may apply to the Tribunal for a direction requiring HMRC to give closure notice within a specified period, such application to be heard and determined in the same way as an appeal. The Tribunal must give the direction unless satisfied that there are reasonable grounds for not giving closure notice within a specified period. [*TMA 1970, s 28A; FA 2015, Sch 7 para 44*].

See **5.2** APPEALS for right of appeal against any conclusion stated or amendment made by a closure notice.

Where an enquiry is to be concluded by means of a contract settlement (see **6.8** ASSESSMENTS) HMRC do not normally issue a closure notice. A notice will be issued only if the taxpayer or agent insist. (HMRC Enquiry Manual EM6001).

An application for judicial review of a closure notice was unsuccessful in *R (oao Archer) v HMRC QB,* [2017] EWHC 296 (Admin), 2017 STI 328. The notice did not state the tax dues and was therefore defective. However, the taxpayer should have challenged the notice by making an appeal. If an appeal had been made the Tribunal would have cured the defect in the notice by applying *TMA 1970, s 114(1)* (see **6.2** ASSESSMENTS).

Partial closure notices

Legislation will be included in the 2017 Finance Bill so that HMRC and taxpayers will be able to conclude discrete matters in an enquiry into an income tax or corporation tax self-assessment return (and, in due course, the equivalent digital obligation) where more than one issue is open. This will be done by issuing a new partial closure notice (PCN) ahead of the final closure of an enquiry. HMRC will be able to issue a PCN either in agreement with the taxpayer, at their own discretion, or when directed to do so by the First-tier Tax Tribunal on application by a taxpayer.

HMRC will use the new power in cases where there is tax avoidance, high complexity, or where a large amount of tax is at risk. Where HMRC issue a partial closure notice and amend a person's tax return, the taxpayer will have a right to appeal and ask for payment of the tax to be postponed. Tax repayments arising from a PCN need not automatically be repaid, e.g. where tax is due in respect of other issues not covered by the PCN.

The legislation will come into effect from Royal Assent to the Finance Act 2017 and will apply both to enquiries open at that time, and to future enquiries.

For details, see www.gov.uk/government/publications/tax-enquiries-closure-rules.'

65

Social Investment Relief

Introduction

[65.1] The paragraph immediately before the heading 'Meaning of Periods A and B' is replaced by the following.

'As announced at Autumn Statement 2016 the following changes are expected to be made to social investment relief with effect from 6 April 2017—

(a) the investment limit for qualifying social enterprises aged up to seven years old will increase to £1.5m;

(b) nursing homes and residential care homes will be classed as excluded activities, although the government intends to revisit these activities in future with the aim of introducing an accreditation system which will allow fundraising via social investment relief. Also, certain activities, including asset leasing and on-lending, are to be excluded to ensure the scheme is well targeted;

(c) the limit on the number of full-time equivalent employees will be reduced from 500 to 250;

(d) money raised by the social investment relief is not to be used to repay existing loans;

(e) individuals will be eligible to claim relief under the social investment relief only if they are independent from the social enterprise; and

(f) a provision will be introduced to exclude investments where arrangements are put in place with the main purpose of delivering a benefit to an individual or party connected to the social enterprise.

Draft regulations are expected by the end of January 2017.

See also www.gov.uk/government/publications/finance-bill-2017-draft-legislati on-overview-documents/overview-of-legislation-in-draft para 2.11.'

66

Substantial Shareholdings of Companies

Introduction

[66.1] The following text is added at the end.

'Future developments

A number of changes are to be made to the conditions which must be met for the substantial shareholdings exemption to apply, with effect for disposals on or after 1 April 2017. The changes are as follows:

(a) the condition that the investing company must be a trading company or part of a trading group will be removed;

(b)   the condition that the investment must have been held for at least a continuous period of 12 months in the 2 years preceding the sale will be extended to a continuous period of 12 months in the 6 years preceding the sale; and

(c)   the condition that the company whose shares are sold continues to be a qualifying company immediately after the sale will be withdrawn, except where the sale is to a connected party.

The exemption will also apply where the company whose shares are sold is not a trading company if it is owned by qualifying institutional investors (as defined). Full exemption will apply if at least 80 per cent of the ordinary share capital is owned by such investors. Proportionate exemption will apply where between 25 per cent and 80 per cent is owned by such investors.

In addition, where the exemption relating to companies owned by qualifying institutional investors applies, the substantial shareholding condition may be met if the investing company's shareholding is below 10 per cent of the ordinary share capital but cost more than £50 million.

See www.gov.uk/government/publications/reform-of-substantial-shareholding -exemption-for-qualifying-institutional-investors.'

Spring Budget 2017

This is a summary of the most important tax changes in Spring Budget 2017. For more on the Budget, see the Spring Budget 2017 report and the Overview of tax legislation and rates 2017 ('OOTLAR') published by HM Treasury and HMRC (www.gov.uk/Government/publications/spring-budget-2017-overview -of-tax-legislation-and-rates-ootlar).

Personal and Business Tax

The highlights for individuals from the Spring Budget 2017 include:

- the making tax digital threshold for a one-year deferral in digital quarterly reporting will be the VAT threshold,
- the reduction in the dividend nil-rate band from £5,000 to £2,000 in 2018/19,
- the extension of the opportunity to clean-up mixed funds held by non-domiciliaries to cover pre-6 April 2008 foreign income and capital,
- a 25% tax charge on pension transfers to a qualifying recognised overseas pension scheme (QROPS) which take place on or after 9 March 2017.

Personal tax rates and allowances – 2017/18 tax year

Income tax allowances

Personal allowance	£11,500
Income limit for personal allowance	£100,000
Transferable tax allowance (also known as marriage allowance)	£1,150
Married couple's allowance (born before 6 April 1935)	£8,445
Minimum amount of married couple's allowance	£3,260
Income limit for married couple's allowance	£28,000
Blind person's allowance	£2,320

Income tax rates and taxable bands

Rate	
Starting rate for savings: 0%	£1–£5,000
Basic rate: 20%	£1–£33,500
Higher rate: 40%	£33,501–£150,000
Additional rate: 45%	Over £150,000

The savings rates are 0% (starting rate for savings), 0% (savings nil-rate band of £1,000 for basic rate taxpayers and £500 for higher rate taxpayers), 20% (savings basic rate), 40% (savings higher rate), 45% (savings additional rate).

The dividend rates are 0% (dividend nil rate on first £5,000 of dividend income), 7.5% (dividend ordinary rate), 32.5% (dividend upper rate) and 38.1% (dividend additional rate).

In 2017/18 the higher rate will kick in at an income level (before personal allowances) of £45,000 (rather than £43,000 as in 2016/17). This is the biggest above inflation increase to the threshold since it was introduced in 1989.

Scottish taxpayers – income tax bands

The Scottish Government has the power to vary the basic rate, higher rate and additional rate of income tax for non-savings income. It can also create new tax bands. It does not have the power to set the level of the personal allowance, set different rates for different types of income or alter/create/abolish income tax reliefs. These remain reserved by the UK Government.

As was widely expected, the Scottish higher rate threshold (personal allowance plus Scottish basic rate band) in 2017/18 is to be lower than the threshold which applies in the rest of the UK. The Scottish higher rate threshold will be £43,000 in 2017/18 (frozen at the 2016/17 level). The rates of tax and other thresholds remain the same as in the rest of the UK.

This creates a number of mismatches for Scottish taxpayers:

Mismatch	Commentary
Class 1 and Class 4 national insurance contributions	The upper earnings limit for Class 1 and the upper profits limit for Class 4 are aligned with the higher rate threshold which applies in the rest of the UK. Therefore, employed Scottish taxpayers will face a marginal rate of 52% on earnings between £43,000 and £45,000 (Scottish higher rate of 40% plus Class 1 primary rate of 12%). The marginal rate for the self-employed at this profit level will be 49% (Scottish higher rate of 40% plus Class 4 main rate of 9%).
Savings income and dividend income	The income tax rates and thresholds for the savings and dividend income of Scottish taxpayers are the same as for taxpayers in the rest of the UK. This means the starting rate for savings, savings nil-rate band and dividend nil-rate band should be considered for Scottish taxpayers. It also means that Scottish taxpayers may be higher rate taxpayers for non-savings income but basic rate taxpayers for savings income.

Mismatch	Commentary
Rates of capital gains tax	The rate of capital gains tax depends on the remaining basic rate band for income tax. The higher rate threshold for capital gains tax for Scottish taxpayers will remain aligned with the higher rate threshold for the rest of the UK. Therefore it is possible to be a higher rate taxpayer in Scotland but have remaining basic rate band for the purposes of capital gains tax.

National insurance rates and thresholds

Lower earnings limit, primary Class 1	£113
Upper earnings limit, primary Class 1	£866
Primary threshold	£157
Secondary threshold	£157
Upper secondary threshold	£866
Employment allowance (per employer)	£3,000 per year
Employees' primary Class 1 rate between primary threshold and upper earnings limit	12%
Employees' primary Class 1 rate above upper earnings limit	2%
Employers' secondary Class 1 rate above secondary threshold	13.8%
Class 1A rate on employer-provided benefits	13.8%
Class 1B rate on amounts included in a PAYE settlement agreement	13.8%
Class 2 rate	£2.85
Class 2 small profits threshold	£6,025 per year
Class 3 rate	£14.25
Class 4 lower profits limit	£8,164 per year
Class 4 upper profits limit	£45,000 per year
Class 4 rate between lower profits limit and upper profits limit	9%
Class 4 rate above upper profits limit	2%

There is an exemption from secondary Class 1 national insurance contributions (NIC) in relation to employees under 21 and apprentices under 25 years old. The exemption applies until the employee's earnings reach the upper secondary threshold, at which point secondary contributions are due.

Note that the ability to make voluntary Class 3A contributions ceases on 5 April 2017. This was a temporary class of NIC introduced to give people who reached state pension age before 6 April 2016 the opportunity to build up their state pension entitlement by up to £25 per week.

Capital gains tax rates and exempt amount

The annual exempt amount for capital gains tax is increased to £11,300 in 2017/18. The annual exempt amount for trustees in 2017/18 is £5,650.

The capital gains tax rates remain the same for individuals, personal representatives and trustees as they were in 2016/17. The main rates are 10% for basic rate taxpayers and 20% for higher rate taxpayers, trustees and personal representatives. The 'upper rates' of 18% (basic rate taxpayers) and 28% (higher rate taxpayers, trustees and personal representatives) apply to gains on residential property and carried interest. The rate of tax for ATED-related gains remains 28%.

Inheritance tax

The nil-rate band remains £325,000 and the rate of inheritance tax remains unchanged. As announced in Summer Budget 2015, the nil-rate band will remain frozen until 2021/22 at the earliest.

The residence nil-rate band is phased in from 2017/18. The residence nil-rate band applies to reduce the inheritance tax payable on death but is restricted to the value of residential property included in the death estate which is passed to direct descendants.

The amount of the residence nil-rate band available where the date of death falls in 2017/18 is £100,000.

Business owners

Dividend nil rate

Introduced from 2016/17, the dividend nil-rate band (also referred to as the dividend allowance) taxes the first £5,000 of dividend income at 0%, irrespective of the taxpayer's marginal tax rate. At the time it was speculated that this both acted as a simplification measure for the making tax digital agenda and a sweetener for the increase in the effective tax rates for dividend income introduced at the same time.

Given the level of the dividend nil-rate band it is not surprising that the taxpayers who benefitted most from this measure were owner-managers of companies.

As part of the aim to reduce the tax incentive for incorporation, from 2018/19 the dividend nil-rate band will be reduced to £2,000. The Chancellor asserts that at this level most general investors will still pay no tax on their dividends.

It is therefore essential to ensure that individuals maximise their use of the £5,000 dividend nil-rate band in 2017/18.

Appropriations into trading stock

If a trader transfers a business asset into trading stock, the cost of the stock for the purpose of the accounts is the market value at the time it was appropriated. For capital gains purposes, the trader is deemed to have sold the fixed asset at market value. In this instance the trader can elect not to have a capital gains tax disposal but instead to have the cost of the stock reduced by the amount of the chargeable gain. This will reduce the gain to nil but will result in the stock having a lower cost (and therefore a higher trading profit when the stock is eventually sold).

For transfers on or after 8 March 2017, it is no longer possible to make such an election where an allowable loss would arise on an appropriation into trading stock at market value. This means that an allowable loss will be crystallised when the appropriation takes place, and the loss will remain within the capital gains tax rules with respect to how it may be set off in the future. The aim of this provision is to remove the ability of business with loss-making capital assets to obtain an unfair tax advantage by converting those losses into more flexible trading losses.

Where traders have more than one asset they wish to appropriate as trading stock, it will be sensible to consider the timing of this. Where one asset stands at a gain, and one at a loss, it may be advantageous to appropriate the asset standing at a gain before or at the same time as the asset standing at a loss and make no election. This will ensure that the loss arising can be utilised more effectively within the capital gains tax rules.

Partnership tax treatment

Following the August 2016 consultation, Finance Bill 2018 will contain provisions which clarify some aspects of partnership taxation, particularly in relation to profit allocations. The Government is aware that some of the existing rules are unclear or produce an inappropriate outcome and wishes to make both the calculation and reporting of profits simpler. A summary of responses is also expected.

Simplified cash basis for small unincorporated businesses

In line with the summary of responses, with effect from 6 April 2017 the entry and exit thresholds for the simplified cash basis for small unincorporated businesses are being increased. The entry threshold will increase from £83,000 to £150,000. The exit threshold will be £300,000. For Universal Credit claimants both the entry and exit thresholds will be £300,000.

At the same time the rules for deductible capital expenditure under the simplified cash basis will be clarified via the introduction of a statutory list of disallowed expenditure. For 2017/18 profits can be calculated using either the new rules or the existing rules.

Following consultation on the draft legislation, the Finance Bill 2017 clauses will be revised to ensure the rules on the movement from the cash basis to the accruals basis are 'robust'.

Employee issues

Valuation of benefits in kind

As expected from Autumn Statement 2016, the Government will:

- launch a consultation on the valuation of living accommodation,
- publish a call for evidence on the valuation of all other benefits in kind.

Relief for business expenses

A call for evidence will be published in the Finance Bill on the use of income tax relief for employees' business expenses, including those not reimbursed by the employer.

Termination payments

The following changes are to be made to the income tax and NIC treatment of termination payments from 6 April 2018:

- removal of the distinction between the taxation of contractual and non-contractual payments in lieu of notice (PILONs) and make all PILONs both taxable and subject to Class 1 NIC (primary and secondary contributions),
- retention of the £30,000 threshold for termination payments but amounts above that would be subject to secondary Class 1 NIC (no primary Class 1 contributions will be payable by the employee) as well as income tax,
- removal of foreign service relief (except in the case of seafarers).

Although these measures were pre-announced, it is now understood that whilst the bulk of the changes will be legislated in Finance Bill 2017 and NIC Bill 2017 as planned, the abolition of foreign service relief will be deferred to Finance Bill 2018 based on responses to the draft legislation.

Enterprise management incentives

The Government is to seek state aid approval to extend the tax reliefs associated with the enterprise management incentive (EMI) scheme beyond 2018. The last time state aid approval was granted to this scheme was in August 2009.

Property owners

Simplified cash basis for unincorporated businesses

As stated in the January 2017 summary of responses, the simplified cash basis will be extended to unincorporated property businesses from 6 April 2017.

This will be the default method of calculating the property income, unless:

- the landlord makes an election not to use the simplified cash basis (separate elections must be made for different types of property businesses),
- the gross rental income exceeds £150,000,
- the business is carried on by a company, an LLP, a partnership with a corporate partner, a trust or personal representatives,
- business premises renovation allowances have been claimed and there is a balancing adjustment in the tax year.

For those property businesses unwilling or unable to use the simplified cash basis, the accruals basis must be used to calculate the property income.

Where property is owned jointly by spouses or civil partners, if one spouse or civil partner makes an election for the accruals basis to apply then the other spouse/civil partner is excluded from using the simplified cash basis. For all other jointly owned property, each owner can choose whether to elect to use the accruals basis or to remain on the simplified cash basis.

The simplified cash basis for unincorporated property businesses is closely modelled on the simplified cash basis for unincorporated trading businesses, however there are some important differences:

- interest is allowed as a deduction without the application of the £500 limit and the related mixed purpose interest rule (instead interest will be allowed according to the existing rules for landlords, including the restriction of relief for interest in relation to residential properties starting in 2017/18),
- the continued ability to deduct the cost of replacing domestic items in residential properties which applies from 2016/17. The initial cost of capital items used in a dwelling house will not be an allowable expense under the simplified cash basis in the same way as this is not permitted under the accruals basis.

Landlords should consider carefully whether the cash basis is beneficial to them. Whilst simplified accounting may be tempting it could create other issues, particularly in relation to the timing of receipts. For example, if a tenant pays a full year's rent in advance on 31 March then the entire amount must be included in the profits for that year, which could impact areas such as the high income child benefit charge or the abatement of the personal allowance where the adjusted net income exceeds £100,000.

Rent-a-room relief

In a surprise announcement, in summer 2017 the Government will launch a consultation on rent-a-room relief, with a view to better supporting longer-term lodgings.

The reference to longer-term lodging may suggest that the conditions for rent-a-room relief could be altered to ensure it applies to long-term lets only. Currently anyone letting a room in their home on a short-term basis using sharing websites such as Airbnb can receive up to £7,500 per year in rents without paying income tax. When rent-a-room relief was introduced in 1992, this type of short-term letting could not be envisaged and the Government may decide this does not meet the original policy objective.

Non-domiciliaries

At Summer Budget 2015 Chancellor Osborne announced fundamental changes to the tax regime for non-domiciled individuals. They involve deeming an individual to be UK domiciled for tax purposes even though he may be non-domiciled in the UK under general law. The rules will apply for income tax, capital gains tax (CGT) and inheritance tax (IHT).

From 2017/18 it is expected that an individual will be deemed UK domiciled for income tax and CGT:

- if he has been UK resident for at least 15 out of the last 20 tax years, or
- if he was born in the UK with a UK domicile of origin, subsequently left the UK and acquired a non-UK domicile of choice and later becomes resident in the UK

The 20-year 'look-back' period for 2017/18 is 1997/98 to 2016/17. The 'clock' does not restart from 2017/18.

Following the responses to the initial consultation, it was announced that non-domiciliaries:

- caught by the deemed domicile 15-year rule in 2017/18 will be able to rebase their foreign chargeable assets for CGT purposes as at 5 April 2017,
- will have a one-off opportunity to clean-up existing mixed funds within foreign bank accounts (transfers out should be made between 6 April 2017 and 5 April 2019).

Whilst both these measures are good news for the non-domiciliary, they have underlying traps for the unwary that were not obvious at the time of the original announcements.

Clean-up of mixed funds

The change announced affects the cleansing of mixed funds. Based on the latest draft legislation, released on 26 January 2017, it was pointed out by the Chartered Institute of Taxation that mixed funds containing pre-6 April 2008 income and/or capital were excluded from the clean-up. CIOT response (23 Feb 2017), paras 14.6–14.9.

It is confirmed that the Finance Bill 2017 clauses will be amended to include such mixed funds within the opportunity. This probably reflects the original policy intention, since excluding such mixed funds would severely limit its usefulness.

However several uncertainties remain, including: (i) whether it will be possible to clean-up mixed funds based on reasonable estimates of foreign income and capital rather than absolute certainty and (ii) how to determine the composition of any funds remaining in the original bank account following the transfers out. Whilst it is possible that this may be ironed out in the Finance Bill 2017 clauses due for publication on 20 March 2017, it is likely that others will be covered in the subsequent HMRC guidance. Some advisers may, therefore, decide to wait for the publication of the HMRC guidance before beginning to split out mixed funds. The fact that the time limit has been extended to 5 April 2019 (from the originally proposed deadline of 5 April 2018) is helpful here.

Pensions

Money purchase annual allowance

As announced in Autumn Statement 2016, the money purchase annual allowance (MPAA) will be reduced from £10,000 to £4,000. The MPAA is only triggered when a pension scheme member draws income from a flexi-access drawdown fund and it exists to prevent the member reinvesting this money back into a pension, thus obtaining double income tax relief.

Note that the MPAA is **not** triggered if:

* the member uses the tax-free lump sum only and does not draw income from the taxable portion of the fund,
* the member's fund is still held under the former 'capped drawdown' arrangement and the withdrawals of income do not exceed the capped amount (if the cap is exceeded, the drawdown fund automatically converts to flexi-access in any case).

Provided members can keep their withdrawals within these conditions, the standard annual allowance of £40,000 applies.

The summary of responses to the November 2016 consultation was expected to be published on 20 March 2017.

Foreign pensions

The announcement at Autumn Statement 2016 that the tax treatment of foreign pensions would be 'more closely aligned' with the UK's domestic pension tax regime was broadly interpreted as being notice that the rule under which only 90% of foreign pension income is subject to UK income tax would be abolished. This was confirmed as correct by the draft legislation published in December 2016.

Specialist schemes for those employed abroad (known as 'section 615' schemes) will be closed to new saving but any lump sums paid out in relation to funds built up before 6 April 2017 will be subject to the current tax treatment.

Foreign pensions – QROPS

A 25% tax charge will be levied on pension transfers to a qualifying recognised overseas pension scheme (QROPS) which take place on or after 9 March 2017.

Although the legitimate use of QROPS is acknowledged, it is noted that the transfer of funds which have benefited from UK income tax relief has provided an opportunity for a tax advantage. QROPS can be located in a lower tax jurisdiction or one which offers less restrictive withdrawal rules. As a result, QROPS schemes have been marketed as tax saving vehicles. The new law aims to preserve the legitimate purpose of transferring pension schemes, whilst penalising the tax avoidance motive.

'Genuine' transfers will be identified if they meet one of the following conditions:

- the QROPS and the person who makes the transfer are resident in the same country, or
- the QROPS and the person who makes the transfer are both resident in a country within the European Economic Area, or
- the transfer is made to a QROPS that is established or sponsored by the employer of the person who makes the transfer.

Transfers which do not meet these conditions will incur a charge of 25% of the value of the transferred.

There will be a five-year window following the transfer during which:

- a transfer which was not chargeable will become so if it ceases to meet the qualifying conditions regarding residence, and
- a charge which was made can be refunded if one of the qualifying conditions starts to apply,
- payments out of the QROPS will be subject to UK tax rules regardless of where the individual then resides.

The administrators of both the UK scheme and the QROPS will be jointly and severally liable to the tax charge. It is expected that it will be deducted from the pension fund on transfer.

Tax planning with QROPS is a niche area, popular with wealthy and internationally mobile individuals. Advisers with clients who may be affected by these changes are advised to study the draft legislation and HMRC guidance at an early stage in view of the immediate changes in the law. Existing QROPS have an early deadline of 13 April 2017 to decide whether they wish to maintain their status.

Investments

ISAs

The ISA limit will be £20,000 in 2017/18 (up from £15,420 in 2016/17), as previously trailed in Budget 2016. The Chancellor used this above inflation increase to partly justify his reduction to the dividend nil-rate band; individuals can purchase shares via an ISA to benefit from the tax-free wrapper.

Venture capital schemes

As announced in Autumn Statement 2016, further minor tweaks to the rules for enterprise investment schemes (EIS), venture capital trusts (VCTs) and seed enterprise investment schemes (SEIS) are expected in Finance Bill 2017:

- clarification to the rules for share conversion rights (for EIS and SEIS shares issued on or after 5 December 2016), which means that the 'no pre-arranged exits' requirement will not apply if a right exists for the conversion or exchange of shares at some future date,
- aligning the VCT rules for follow-on funding to match the rules for EIS,
- a power to enable the rules on share-for-share exchanges for VCTs to be made via secondary legislation.

The summary of responses to the December 2015 consultation on ways of improving the advance assurance service for venture capital schemes is expected to follow the Spring Budget 2017.

Social investments tax relief

As partially announced in Autumn Statement 2016 and further to the draft legislation published on 26 January 2017, the following changes to social investments tax relief (SITR) will apply to investments made on or after 6 April 2017:

- the investment limit for qualifying social enterprises aged up to seven years old will increase to £1.5m,
- the list of excluded activities will be tightened up to include asset leasing and on-lending. Whilst nursing homes and residential care homes will also be classed as excluded activities, the Government intends to revisit these activities in future with the aim of introducing an accreditation system which will allow fundraising via SITR,
- the limit on the number of full-time equivalent employees will be reduced from 500 to 250,
- the use of money raised under the SITR to pay off existing loans will be excluded,
- the law will be clarified so that individuals will be eligible to claim relief under the SITR only if they are independent from the social enterprise,
- a provision will be introduced to exclude investments where arrangements are put in place with the main purpose of delivering a benefit to an individual or party connected to the social enterprise.

Life insurance policies

As expected, legislation will be introduced in Finance Bill 2017 to change the taxation of partial surrenders from life insurance policies in order to prevent excessive tax charges. However, it is interesting that despite consulting on three options, in the end the draft legislation published in December 2016 contained a remedy which was not mentioned in the consultation. Any policy holder who has inadvertently triggered a disproportionate gain will be able to apply to HMRC to have the chargeable event gain recalculated on a just and reasonable basis.

However, the fact that the draft legislation was built around an option which had not been subject to consultation meant that uncertainties remained over the operation of the provision. As such, following comments received, the Finance Bill 2017 clauses will be revised to clarify who can apply, when the application can be made and how the recalculation is to be given effect. These rules will apply from Royal Assent to Finance Act 2017.

Whether this will address the other concerns raised, such as the lack of a statutory right of appeal, remains to be seen.

Savings bonds

As expected, National Savings and Investments (NS&I) will launch a new three-year savings bond in April 2017. It was confirmed in the Spring Budget 2017 that the interest rate will be 2.2% per annum. The bond will be open to those over 16 years of age and the maximum investment will be £3,000. This interest rate is significantly higher than the rates offered by banks and building societies for mainstream savings products and there is likely to be a high take-up amongst basic rate and higher rate taxpayers (who also benefit from the savings nil-rate band).

Administration

Making tax digital

Under making tax digital, businesses will be required to file quarterly income and expense reports digitally. For many businesses this will represent significant extra administration work plus the cost of buying an appropriate software package and extra accountancy fees.

Based on the threshold for the one-year deferral announced in Spring Budget 2017, the main timescales for mandation will be:

- April 2018 – unincorporated businesses (including unincorporated property businesses) with a turnover above the VAT registration threshold (for their income tax obligations only),
- April 2019 – unincorporated businesses (including unincorporated property businesses) with a turnover above £10,000 but below the VAT registration threshold (for their income tax obligations) **plus** all businesses (unincorporated and incorporated) for their VAT obligations,
- April 2020 – all incorporated businesses for their corporation tax obligations.

The use of the VAT threshold as the level for the one-year deferral of quarterly digital reporting is a significant and very welcome development. Anecdotal evidence suggested that HMRC had been reluctant to entertain the idea of using the VAT threshold during the consultation process and it is to its credit that it has listened to advisers on this matter.

For unincorporated businesses it is expected that these requirements will apply to the accounting period beginning on or after 6 April of the relevant year. Therefore, for unincorporated trading businesses it may be possible to extend the deferral period by changing their accounting date. For example a business with turnover below the VAT threshold and an accounting date of 31 March will not have to make quarterly digital reports until the accounting period beginning 1 April 2020. Consideration should of course be given to the change of accounting date rules.

It is not possible to change the accounting date for an unincorporated property business as the income must be reported on a tax year basis.

Making tax digital – tax administration

A further consultation on late submission penalties under the making tax digital regime was due to be published on 20 March 2017.

At the same time, the Government will also consult on the 'design aspects of the tax administration system', with the aim of a consistent approach across the taxes. However it would appear from the draft legislation on administration published in January 2017 that we can expect amendments to be made to the existing statutes rather than using making tax digital as an opportunity for a total rethink of tax administration from a 21st Century perspective.

NIC – collection of arrears

It was announced at Autumn Statement 2016 that from April 2018 NIC would no longer be covered by the Limitation Act 1980. However, this is now expected to be delayed to allow for full consultation. Currently if HMRC wants to recover NIC debt it must raise a protective assessment within six years of the end of the tax year in question. The collection of arrears of tax is not covered by the Limitation Act 1980 so this leads to a mismatch in dealing with historic tax investigations where there is an associated NIC liability.

This is an interesting measure as it will enable HMRC to collect more NIC arrears, but by aligning the treatment for tax and NIC it means it can be badged as a simplification measure and a step towards income tax and NIC alignment.

Note that the position in Scotland is different. There it is already possible to collect NIC debt going back 20 years.

Income tax allowances for property and trading income

The £1,000 'allowances' for property and trading income, previously announced in Budget 2016, come into force in 2017/18. The trading income allowance also covers miscellaneous income from the provision of assets or services.

These work in a similar way to rent-a-room relief in that the first £1,000 of gross trading or property income will be exempt from income tax. If the income exceeds £1,000 the taxpayer will have a choice of:

- deducting the £1,000 'allowance' from their gross income and being taxable on the excess, or
- deducting allowable expenses in the normal way.

To utilise the allowance, the individual must make an election by the first anniversary of 31 January after the end of the tax year (e.g. 31 January 2020 for the 2017/18 tax year).

However, following consultation on the draft legislation published in December 2016, changes will be made in Finance Bill 2017 to prevent the allowances from applying to:

- the income of a participator in a connected close company,
- partnership income.

Employment Taxes

Both generally and from the perspective of employers and their advisers, the spring Budget was refreshingly light on tax measures. Details of those which were included can be found in Chapter 3 of the Spring Budget 2017 document and supported by the OOTLAR which summarises all changes in the pipeline, including those previously announced.

Company cars

There were no changes announced to the company car tax rates that will apply from 2017/18 to 2020/21 as already either enacted or announced in the Autumn Statement.

National Living Wage/National Minimum Wage

The Chancellor in the Budget announced that the National Living Wage will be increased to £7.50 per hour from April 2017. The following table shows all minimum wage rates for all age groups:

Category	Current rate	New rate from 1 April 2017
Workers 25 and over	£7.20 per hour	£7.50 per hour
21–24 year olds	£6.95 per hour	£7.05 per hour
18–20 year olds	£5.55 per hour	£5.60 per hour
16–17 year olds	£4.00 per hour	£4.05 per hour
Apprentices	£3.40 per hour	£3.50 per hour
Accommodation offset	£6.00 per day	£6.40 per day

Personal service companies ('IR35')

As announced in last year's Budget, as from 6 April 2017, where a worker provides his services through a personal service company (PSC) to a public sector body, it will be up to the public sector body (or the agency responsible for paying the PSC) to decide whether or not the special rules for PSCs (known as the IR35 rules) should apply. If the IR35 rules do apply, then the public sector body or agency will deduct the tax due on the resulting deemed employment income payment from the amount due to the PSC under the contract.

In a recent change to proposals for how the public sector body (or agency) should calculate the deemed employment payment, it will be up to them whether they take account of the worker's expenses in calculating that amount. If the expenses are left out of account the worker could still claim a deduction for qualifying expenses in the normal way.

The outline of this measure is covered in HMRC's tax information and impact note.

The list of public bodies who will assume this new responsibility as from 6 April was included as Annex B to the consultation document on this change in approach.

HMRC has also recently published a revised Employment Status Tool to help anyone considering the position of a worker providing services through a PSC to decide whether or not the IR35 rules apply.

Dividend nil-rate band reduction

In a step ostensibly aimed at addressing the unfairness in the differences in tax treatment between employees and those who provide their services through a limited company, the Chancellor announced that the dividend nil-rate band will reduce from £5,000 to £2,000 from 6 April 2018. Although this will indeed impact on the users of personal service companies, it will have a wider impact, affecting anyone receiving dividends of over £2,000 a year, including shareholder directors/employees of many smaller companies.

Pensions

The Budget did not include any new proposals in respect of the lifetime allowance or annual allowance for pension contributions.

However, employers of internationally mobile employees may well want to be aware that there is a new 25% charge on pension scheme members if they make a transfer from a UK-registered pension scheme to a Qualifying Recognised Overseas Pension Scheme (QROPS). It will apply to transfers taking place on or after 9 March 2017. This charge does not apply if **any** of the following apply:

- the member is resident in the same country in which the QROPS receiving the transfer is established,
- the member is resident in a country within the European Economic Area (EEA) and the QROPS is established in a country within the EEA,

- the QROPS is an occupational pension scheme sponsored by the individual's employer,
- the QROPS is an overseas public service pension scheme and the member is an employee of an employer that participates in the scheme,
- the QROPS is set up by an international organisation to provide benefits for or in respect of past service as an employee of the organisation and the member is an employee of that international organisation.

This means that an employee making a transfer from a registered scheme into a QROPS as a consequence of a cross-border change in employment will often be outside the new charge.

Other changes to be included in Finance Bill 2017

The OOTLAR document includes confirmation that a number of previously announced measures of particular interest to employers are still on course to be included in Finance Bill 2017.

Benefits in kind

During the summer last year there was a consultation on proposals to align the date for 'making good' on benefits in kind. If an employee 'makes good' (repays) an amount to the employer in respect of a benefit in kind, the cash equivalent is reduced by the amount made good. The date by which the employee must 'make good' in order to reduce a benefit varies according to the benefit provided.

In para 1.6 of OOTLAR, HMRC confirms that Finance Bill 2017 will include legislation to set the aligned date to be 6 July following the end of the tax year. This change will apply for benefits provided in 2017/18 onwards.

Salary sacrifice

With effect from 6 April 2017, salary sacrifice arrangements, described as 'optional remuneration arrangements', may be used to achieve tax and NIC savings only in the case of:

- employer pension contributions and advice,
- employer-provided childcare,
- cycle-to-work schemes,
- ultra-low emission company cars.

Transitional provisions apply where the salary sacrifice arrangement was in place before 6 April 2017. See para 1.7 of OOTLAR.

Termination payments

The Autumn Statement last year included details of the expected changes to the treatment of termination payments. In para 1.8 of today's OOTLAR, HMRC indicates that although the main changes to the tax and NIC treatment of termination payments will be legislated in the Finance Bill 2017, proposals to abolish foreign service relief will be deferred to the Finance Bill 2018.

Proposal dropped – sanction for hiring illegal workers

In last year's Budget the Chancellor announced an intention to temporarily deny the NIC employment allowance to employers taking on workers who do not have a legal right to work in the UK. Following consultation, this proposal has been dropped. Any employer taking on such workers already faces significant civil penalties of up to £20,000 per illegal worker.

Upcoming consultations

The OOTLAR document gives details of a number of consultations on possible future changes to employment taxes, due to be published on 20 March 2017:

- a call for evidence on employees' expenses,
- consultation on proposal to modernise the tax treatment of employer-provided living accommodation and board and lodgings

a call for evidence on exemptions and valuation methodology for employer-provided benefits in kind.

Corporation Tax

In the spirit of moving towards a single fiscal event in the autumn, the Spring Budget 2017 does not set out major changes to the taxation of companies. Minor amendments have been made to a number of announcements made in previous years, details of which are provided below.

Further information on some of the announcements will be available when the Finance Bill 2017 is published.

Appropriations to trading stock

Currently, if a fixed asset is appropriated into trading stock, then the 'cost' of the stock for the purposes of the accounts is the market value at the time it was introduced. For chargeable gains purposes, there is a deemed disposal of the fixed asset at market value. In this instance an election can be made to reduce the cost of the stock by the amount of the chargeable gain, rather than triggering a disposal. This will reduce the gain to nil but will result in the stock having a lower cost, and therefore a higher trading profit, when the stock is eventually sold.

For transfers made on or after 8 March 2017, it is no longer possible to make such an election where an allowable loss would arise on an appropriation into trading stock at market value. This means that an allowable loss will be crystallised when the appropriation takes place, and the loss will remain within the chargeable gains rules with respect to how it may be set off in the future. The aim of this provision is to remove the ability of businesses with loss making capital assets to obtain an unfair tax advantage by converting those losses into more flexible trading losses.

Where companies have more than one asset that may be appropriated to trading stock, it will be sensible to consider the timing of any appropriation. Where one asset stands at a gain, and one at a loss, it may be advantageous to appropriate the asset standing at a gain before or at the same time as the asset standing at a loss and make no election. This will ensure that the loss arising can be utilised more effectively within the chargeable gains rules.

Review of R&D regime

The UK has a comprehensive regime to encourage companies to invest in research and development.

Following a review, the Government has announced that administrative changes will be made to the research and development expenditure credit (RDEC) to increase certainty and to simplify claims. Action will also be taken to increase awareness of R&D tax credits among SMEs. Further details on the changes, or indeed when they are likely to have effect, have not been provided.

Offshore property developers

Legislation was introduced by Finance Act 2016, ss 76–77 to ensure non-resident developers of UK land are subject to UK corporation tax on the profits generated by this activity. This was intended to create a level playing field between UK and foreign-based developers. The original legislation excluded profits arising from contracts entered into before 5 July 2016. The Government did not anticipate that profits arising many months or years later as a result of these contracts would not be subject to UK corporation tax. Amendments have been made to ensure that all profits recognised in a period of account beginning on or after 8 March 2017 are taxed irrespective of when the contract was entered into. Where the period of account straddles 8 March 2017, then the amounts arising between 8 March 2017 and the end of the straddling period are also taxed.

Plant and machinery leasing

Current rules under GAAP treat leased assets as either finance leases or operating leases. Finance leases are capitalised on the balance sheet as fixed assets, with a matching lease obligation in creditors. Assets subject to operating leases are off balance sheet assets.

IFRS 16, which is the new leasing standard issued by the International Accounting Standards Board, comes into effect on 1 January 2019. This standard will radically alter the GAAP treatment of lessees of most assets, although lessors will still maintain a distinction between finance and operating leases. There are exceptions within the standard for leases of 12 months or less and low value items.

The impact for lessees will be to increase the level of debt and the value of the asset base on the balance sheet, as all leases must be capitalised. The timing of debits recognised in the accounts on operating leases will be accelerated, even though the payments for hire of the asset are likely to be uniform over the lease. Rental expenses on leases which are currently classified as operating leases will be replaced by depreciation and front loaded interest charges. Companies using IFRS may need to model the effect on their gearing, earnings per share and debt covenants as well as many other financial metrics and ratios.

The Government will launch a consultation in Summer 2017, building on the discussion document published in Summer 2016. The Government intends to maintain the current system of lease taxation, rather than changing the tax system to match the accounting. This would seem to be the most sensible approach as it should avoid awkward and complex transitional adjustments. However, one downside of this approach will be to create differences between the P&L debits and the amounts deductible for tax, requiring greater measurement and tracking of temporary differences within deferred tax.

It should be noted that some changes to the rules on long funding leases and certain anti-avoidance rules on leasing will be required as they are linked to current accounting definitions.

Withholding tax amendments

Withholding tax exemption for debt traded on multilateral trading facility

UK tax at the basic rate of 20% must be withheld from certain payments of annual interest. It was announced that an exemption will be introduced for interest on debt traded on a multilateral trading facility. The purpose of the exemption, which is subject to consultation in Spring 2017, is to further the development of UK debt markets.

Double taxation treaty passport scheme

HMRC launched a Double Taxation Treaty Passport (DTTP) scheme for overseas corporate lenders applicable to loans taken out on or after 1 September 2010. The lender must be resident in a country with which the UK has a double taxation treaty that includes an interest or income from a debt claim article. The existence of a 'Treaty Passport' simplifies the process whereby a UK borrower is able to access reduced rates of withholding tax. In order to assist businesses with raising finance, the Government announced today an intention to renew and extend the administrative simplifications of the DTTP scheme. Guidance and the revised terms and conditions applying to the scheme will be published on GOV.UK on 6 April 2017.

Large business risk review

A consultation document is due to be published in Summer 2017 which aims to review HMRC's processes for assessing the risk profile of large businesses. The Government also wants to consider ways of promoting stronger compliance. Unfortunately, further details have not been provided alongside today's announcement.

Patient capital

'Patient capital' is a term used to describe a long-term capital investment in a growing innovative business. The investor is willing to make a financial investment in a business with no expectation of generating a quick profit, however it is possible that more substantial returns will be generated at some point in the future.

The Patient Capital Review was launched by HM Treasury and the Department for Business, Energy & Industrial Strategy (BEIS) in January 2017 as part of the Government's aim to build a modern industrial strategy. The review did not previously include consideration of the tax measures linked with patient capital for growing businesses. The Chancellor announced today that a consultation will be launched in Spring 2017, which will review the tax reliefs aimed at encouraging investment and entrepreneurship. Specific reliefs have not been mentioned, but it is assumed that it could include EIS reliefs, SEIS reliefs, VCT reliefs, entrepreneurs' relief and investors' relief.

The final recommendations from the review will be presented to the Chancellor ahead of Autumn Budget 2017.

Creative sector tax reliefs

It was confirmed today that the Government will seek State Aid approval for the continued provision of high-end television, animation and video games tax reliefs beyond 2018.

Amendments to measures previously announced

A number of measures that have been announced in the past are subject to minor amendments. Details are provided below.

Deductibility of interest

Following announcements at Budget 2016, plus a period of consultation, draft legislation was published on 5 December 2016 and 26 January 2017 to restrict the tax deduction available to companies in respect of interest and similar items.

From 1 April 2017, a group will have its interest expense restricted to a maximum deduction of 30% of earnings before interest, tax, depreciation and amortisation (EBITDA) that is taxable in the UK. The legislation also includes a modified debt cap replacing the existing worldwide debt cap to ensure that the UK net interest deduction cannot exceed the total net interest expense of the worldwide group. An optional group ratio rule based on the net interest to EBITDA ratio of the worldwide group may result in a greater deduction in some circumstances.

Alternative rules apply to infrastructure companies which may have the effect of largely taking them outside the rules with no interest restriction even though they may be highly geared.

Groups with net interest expense of £2m or less will be unaffected by these rules.

The Government has announced a series of detailed amendments to eliminate 'unintended consequences' and reduce 'unnecessary compliance burdens' as follows:

- changes to the modified debt cap to prevent certain restrictions for carried forward interest expenses,
- the alternative rules for public infrastructure groups will be simplified to eliminate the need to compare levels of indebtedness of non-qualifying group companies. Transitional rules will apply in the first year to allow any necessary restructuring to obtain the more favourable alternative treatment,
- the rules on guaranteed debt have been amended including those in relation to intra-group guarantees,
- income and expenses from dealing in financial instruments will be included in the definition of interest for banking trades,
- special rules will allow insurers to compute interest on an amortised cost basis as an alternative to fair value accounting.

These changes will be reflected in Finance Bill 2017 and will have effect from 1 April 2017.

Reform of the substantial shareholdings exemption (SSE)

Following a period of consultation, amendments will be made to the SSE reforms included in the draft Finance Bill 2017, which were originally announced at Autumn Statement 2016. Whilst we do not yet have details, the latest changes are expected to provide further clarity and certainty and take effect from 1 April 2017.

Reform of loss relief

Reforms to the loss relief regime were originally announced at Budget 2016. Legislation was included in the draft Finance Bill 2017, with further draft legislation published on 26 January 2017. The latest changes include provisions for oil and gas companies and oil contractors. All reforms take effect from 1 April 2017.

Patent box

It was announced at Autumn Statement 2016 that the patent box rules would be revised by Finance Bill 2017 where two or more companies work in collaboration on R&D projects under a cost-sharing arrangement. The definition of a cost-sharing arrangement will be narrowed and the way in which payments are structured under the cost-sharing arrangement will be altered. The changes will take effect from 1 April 2017.

Hybrid mismatches

FA 2016 introduced legislation to tackle aggressive tax planning involving the use of hybrid and other mismatch arrangements. It was announced in a technical note at Autumn Statement 2016 that two minor amendments would be made to the hybrid mismatch rules, and a TIIN has been published providing further details. The first change helps to relieve the administrative compliance burden in respect of financial instruments and the second change ensures that amortisation deductions are not treated as giving rise to a mismatch. The changes take effect from 1 January 2017.

Grassroots sports

It was originally announced at Autumn Statement 2015 that companies will be able to claim a deduction for contributions to grassroots sports in certain circumstances. It was announced today that the treatment of a sport governing body will be extended by Finance Bill 2017 to include its 100% subsidiaries. These provisions will have effect from 1 April 2017.

Tax relief for museums and galleries

As announced at Budget 2016, Finance Bill 2017 will introduce a new tax relief for museums and galleries. Further details on the operation of the relief were announced at Autumn Statement 2016. Following consultation on the legislation contained in draft Finance Bill 2017, it was announced today that the relief will be extended to allow for exhibitions which have a live performance as part of the exhibition, provided the live performance is not the main focus.

Corporation tax in Northern Ireland

For a number of years, the Government has been working with the Northern Ireland Executive to pursue the introduction of an Northern Ireland corporation tax rate of 12.5% from April 2018. It was confirmed today that all small and medium-sized enterprises trading in Northern Ireland will be given the potential to benefit. Anti-abuse provisions together with other minor drafting improvements will feature in the revised legislation contained in Finance Bill 2017.

Inheritance Tax, Trusts and Estates

The Spring Budget was light on new tax proposals overall, and inheritance tax did not feature at all. However, it is worth being reminded of some new measures due to be introduced with effect from April 2017 which have been previously announced and the budget included some new points relating to pensions and trusts which will be of interest to private client practitioners.

Trusts default rate of income tax

The OOTLAR, para 1.1 makes a somewhat cryptic reference to a 'default rate' of income tax which will apply to trustees. This is not a new rate of tax for trusts but requires some explanation.

With effect from 6 April 2017, the Scottish parliament will be able to set a Scottish rate of income tax to apply to non-savings, and non-dividend income in Scotland. This 'main rate' of tax will apply to individuals' employment, trade, pensions and property income. It does not apply to trusts.

To correspond with the creation of a main rate for Scottish taxpayers, the same term will apply to the non-savings, non-dividend income of individuals in the rest of the UK. The inference is, of course, that the main rates for each part of the UK could diverge in due course.

The regional authority over tax rates does not extend to the standard rates applied to trusts or non-residents. Hence the introduction of a new term, 'default rate' which describes the standard rate applied to non-savings, non-dividend income of those entities. For trusts, this category is primarily property income.

Although no additional measures are proposed at present, the separation of the rates does pave the way for different rates for trusts in the future.

Inheritance tax and the non-domicile rules

Practitioners are reminded that the Finance Bill 2017 will legislate for the reform of the domicile rules which was initially outlined in the Summer Budget 2015. The new rules will take effect from 6 April 2017. Draft legislation was published in January 2017 and the OOTLAR, para 1.26 confirmed that the measures will go ahead with only minor amendment. For inheritance tax purposes, the key changes are:

*   a non-UK domiciled person (non-dom) will become deemed domiciled after being UK resident for 15 of the past 20 years (instead of 17 years out of 20 currently),
*   a person with a UK domicile of origin who has acquired a different domicile of choice will be deemed domiciled while they are UK resident,
*   inheritance tax will be charged on all UK residential property even when held by a non-dom through an offshore structure.

The standard non-dom tax planning strategy of placing foreign property in a non-UK resident trust before the individual becomes deemed domiciled continues to be an effective way of minimising UK tax, and is, in fact specifically confirmed in the OOTLAR and draft legislation. However, this strategy will no longer work for a non-dom who had a UK domicile of origin but becomes deemed domiciled when UK resident.

Inheritance tax and residence nil-rate band

For deaths after 6 April 2017 an increase in the nil-rate band will be available where the value of a residence is bequeathed to direct descendants.

VAT, other Indirect Taxes and Duties

VAT

Registration and deregistration thresholds

With effect from the 1 April 2017 the following thresholds will apply:

*   VAT registration threshold will increase from £83,000 to £85,000.
*   The VAT registration threshold for relevant acquisitions from other EU member states will also increase from £83,000 to £85,000.
*   The VAT deregistration threshold will increase from £81,000 to £83,000.

Use and enjoyment provisions for business to consumer mobile phone services

The Government stated that it intends to remove the use and enjoyment provisions that alleviate the need for UK VAT to be charged on business to consumer (B2C) mobile phone services provided to a UK resident person travelling outside of the EU.

The change is intended to resolve the inconsistency where UK VAT is applied to mobile phones used by UK residents when in the EU, but not when the mobile phone is used outside the EU.

The changes are intended to prevent telecommunication providers from using the inconsistency to avoid accounting for UK VAT and it will bring the UK into line with the internationally agreed approach.

Secondary legislation and a TIIN will be published before the summer recess.

Fraud in the provision of labour in the construction sector

The Government announced that it intends to have a consultation on possible options to combat missing trader fraud in the provision of labour in the construction sector. One option would be to extend the scope of the domestic reverse charge mechanism to include labour provided in the construction industry so that the recipient accounts for any VAT due.

A consultation document will be published on 20 March 2017.

Split payment model

Certain overseas businesses avoid paying UK VAT on goods supplied online which undercuts UK retailers and abuses the trust of UK customers purchasing goods via an online marketplace.

The Government had previously announced the introduction of measures that are intended to combat VAT avoidance by online businesses in Autumn Statement 2016. The Government has now announced that it would like to collect evidence on whether it would be appropriate to introduce a new VAT collection mechanism in respect of online sales using technology that enables VAT to be collected and remitted directly to HMRC at the time the sale takes place.

This is commonly referred to as the split payment method, where the supplier will receive the net amount and the VAT will be remitted directly to HMRC. The Government believes that this will be another step that could be used to tackle VAT avoidance by overseas online suppliers selling goods to UK consumers.

A 'call for evidence' will be published on 20 March 2017.

Penalty changes in fraud cases

The Government announced in Autumn Statement 2016 that legislation will be included in Finance Bill 2017 introducing a penalty for participating in VAT fraud. The Government consulted on the draft legislation and as a result they have made some minor amendments to improve clarity of the measure and to limit the naming of a company officer to instances where the amount of tax due exceeds £25,000. The new penalty will come into effect from the date of Royal Assent to the Finance Bill.

Energy and transport taxes

Vehicle Excise Duty (VED)

The VED for cars, motorcycles and vans registered before 1 April 2017 will be increased by the Retail Price Index (RPI) with effect from 1 April 2017.

HGV VED and Road User Levy

These rates will be frozen with effect from 1 April 2017. The Government has requested evidence be provided in respect of updating the existing HGV Road User Levy and they will formally issue this request in Spring 2017. The Government also stated that it intends to work with the industry in order to update the levy so that it will reward hauliers that plan their routes efficiently and incentivise hauliers to make efficient use of the roads and improve air quality.

Red diesel

The Government announced that it intends to request evidence on the use of red diesel in order to improve its understanding of eligible industries and their use of red diesel. The Government would specifically like to receive evidence from urban red diesel users.

The call for evidence will be published on 20 March 2017.

Air Passenger Duty (APD)

The rate of APD for the year 2018/19 will increase in line with the RPI. The rates for 2019/20 will be provided in Autumn Budget 2017 in order to give airlines sufficient notice of the increase.

Carbon pricing

The Government announced that it remains committed to carbon pricing in order to assist with decarbonising the power sector. UK prices are currently determined by the EU Emissions Trading System and Carbon Price Support.

With effect from 2021/22, the Government intends to target a total carbon price and will set the specific tax rate at a later date in order to give businesses greater clarity on the total price that they will be required to pay. Further details on carbon prices for the 2020s will be set out at Autumn Budget 2017.

Levy control framework

The Government is aware that it will need to limit the cost for businesses and households as the UK decarbonises its energy supplies. The Levy Control Framework has already been assisting with controlling the costs of low carbon subsidies in recent years and it will be replaced by a revised set of controls. Details of these new controls will be provided later in 2017.

Insurance Premium Tax (IPT)

The Government has reconfirmed its announcement in Autumn Statement 2016 that it will be introducing anti-forestalling measures when the standard rate increases to 12% with effect from June 2017.

The current anti-forestalling legislation is no longer relevant so new legislation will be introduced with effect from 8 March 2017.

Under the anti-forestalling measure:

(a)   businesses will be required to charge the new rate of IPT on a premium received between the announcement and the rate change if the cover under the insurance contract starts on or after the date of the change. This is done by deeming the premium to be received on the date of the rate change. However, this does not apply where it is the insurer's normal commercial practice to receive pre-payments of premiums, and

(b)   businesses will be required to charge the new rate of IPT on a pro-portion of a premium received between the announcement and the rate change if the cover under the insurance contract starts before the rate change and extends until after the first anniversary of the rate change. This is done by deeming a proportion of the premium to be received on the rate change date. That proportion is the amount which relates to the period of cover which runs from the first anniversary. However, this does not apply where it is the insurer's normal commercial practice to issue contracts for periods longer than one year.

Environmental taxes

Aggregates levy

The current rate of £2 per tonne will remain in effect.

Landfill tax

The value of the Landfill Communities Fund (LCF) for 2017/18 will remain unchanged at £39.3m and the cap on contributions made by landfill operators will increase to 5.3%. The current cap will be maintained, subject to consideration of Landfill Tax receipts, continuing progress in reducing the level of unspent funds that are held by environmental bodies and the proportion of the LCF that are spent on administration costs.

The Government announced that it intends to consult on extending the scope of landfill tax to cover illegal waste disposals that are made without the required permit or licence.

Landfill tax – definition of taxable disposal

The Government previously announced at Budget 2016 that legislation will be introduced in Finance Bill 2017, and in secondary legislation, to amend the definition of a taxable disposal for landfill tax. The Government has consulted in the draft legislation and changes have been introduced in order to clarify the tax treatment of material disposed of at landfill sites and give greater certainty to landfill site operators. The draft legislation has been restructured to simplify and improve ease of comprehension. The measure will come into effect after Royal Assent to Finance Act 2017 and the changes will apply to disposals to landfill in England, Wales and Northern Ireland.

Alcohol and tobacco

Alcohol duty rates and bands

The duty rates on beer, cider, wine and spirits will increase by the RPI with effect from 13 March 2017.

The Government announced that it intends to have a consultation on:

(a)   introducing a new duty band for still cider that has a just below 7.5% abv in order to target white ciders, and

(b)   the impact of introducing a new duty band for still wine and made-wine between 5.5 and 8.5% abv.

Tobacco duty rates

The Government has previously announced in Budget 2014 that tobacco duty rates will increase by 2% above RPI inflation and this change will come into effect from 6pm on 8 March 2017.

Minimum Excise Tax

The Government announced that it will be introducing a Minimum Excise Tax for cigarettes that is intended to target the cheapest tobacco and promote fiscal sustainability. The rate will be set at £268.63 per 1,000 cigarettes. The new tax will come into effect from 20 May 2017.

Tobacco: Illicit Trade Protocol – licensing of equipment and the supply chain

Following the announcement made in Autumn Statement 2015 and following technical consultation on the draft legislation produced in December 2016, legislation will be introduced in Finance Bill 2017 that will be intended to control the use and ownership of tobacco manufacturing machinery in the UK. The changes are intended to prevent the illicit manufacture of tobacco products in the UK by introducing powers to establish a licensing regime for this type of machinery. Powers will also be introduced to provide for forfeiture of unlicensed tobacco manufacturing machinery and penalties for failure to comply with the conditions of a licence. The legislation will take effect from the date of Royal Assent.

Heated tobacco products

As announced in Budget 2016 the Government will be consulting on the duty treatment of heated tobacco products. The consultation will be launched on 20 March 2017 and the consultation document should be available on this date.

Soft drinks levy

The levy for sugar that is added to drinks with a total sugar content of at least five grams per 100 millilitres will be set at 18 pence per litre and drinks with a sugar content of at least eight grams will be set at 24 pence per litre. Manufacturers and importers who take reasonable steps to reduce the sugar content will pay less or alleviate the need to pay the levy at all.

Following consultation the legislation has been revised to include a criminal offence for evasion of the levy. Minor amendments have also been made to improve clarity. The levy will take effect from April 2018.

Gaming duty

Gross gaming yield (GGY)

The Government previously announced in Budget 2016 that they will include legislation in Finance Bill 2017 that will raise the GGY bandings for Gaming Duty in line with inflation based on the RPI. The revised GGY will be used to calculate the amount of Gaming Duty due for accounting periods starting on or after 1 April 2017.

Remote gaming duty – freeplays

The Government announced in Budget 2016 that it will include legislation in Finance Bill 2017 to amend the definition of gaming payment and prizes and change the tax treatment of freeplays for remote gaming duty. The Government consulted on the changes and the draft legislation has been amended to ensure that the change is proportionate. The legislation is intended to ensure that freeplays used to participate in remote gaming will have a value as stakes when calculating the dutiable profit of the operator and freeplays given as prizes will not be deductible.

Anti-Avoidance

Promoters of Tax Avoidance Schemes (POTAS)

The Government announced that it intends to introduce new legislation that is intended to ensure that promoters of tax avoidance schemes cannot circumvent the new POTAS regime by reorganising their business to either share control of a promoting business or putting persons between the promoting business and themselves.

Strengthening tax avoidance sanctions and deterrents

The Government previously announced in Autumn Statement 2016 that a new penalty will be introduced in respect of a person who has enabled another person or business to use a tax avoidance arrangement that is later defeated by HMRC. The Government also intends to remove the defence of having relied on non-independent advice as taking reasonable care when HMRC considers whether penalties will be levied on a person or business that has used a tax avoidance arrangement.

The changes relating to reasonable care come into effect at Royal Assent and apply to inaccuracies in documents relating to tax periods which begin on or after 6 April 2017. The penalty for enablers will apply prospectively to enabling activity after Royal Assent.

Disclosure of indirect tax avoidance schemes

The Government announced in Autumn Statement 2016 that legislation will be introduced in Finance Bill 2017 that is intended to strengthen the regime for disclosing indirect tax avoidance arrangements. The provisions will make scheme promoters primarily responsible for disclosing schemes to HMRC and the scope of the legislation will be extended to include all indirect taxes including the Soft Drinks Levy. These measures will become effective from 1 September 2017.